GAME FISH OF THE
ROCKY MOUNTAINS

GAME FISH OF THE
ROCKY MOUNTAINS
A Guide to Identification
and Habitat

by Dr. Michel Pijoan

NORTHLAND PRESS  FLAGSTAFF, ARIZONA

For more specific information on fishing in the Rocky Mountain area, contact the Fish and Game Department of the state in which you are interested.

Division of Wildlife
6060 Broadway
Denver, CO 80216

Fish and Game Department
P.O. Box 25
Boise, ID 83707

Department of Fish and Game
Helena, MT 59601

Department of Fish and Game
Santa Fe, NM 87503

Game and Fish Department
P.O. Box 1539
Cheyenne, WY 82001

Copyright 1985 by Michel Pijoan

All rights reserved. No part of this publication may be reproduced, stored in a retrieval system, or transmitted in any form or by any means, electronic, mechanical, photocopying, recording, or otherwise, without the prior permission of the publisher.

ISBN 0-87358-372-8 Softcover
Library of Congress Catalog Card Number 84-62424
Composed and Printed in the United States of America

This handbook has been written in an effort to answer the many questions that I have been asked during more than sixty years of fly fishing. At the tender age of seventy-four, I decided to assemble this short guidebook for young and old alike who seek bits of information about the fish common to the Rocky Mountain area. I would like to dedicate it to the memory of Edward R. Hewitt and Theodore Gordon.

CONTENTS

ACKNOWLEDGEMENTS

A great many anglers have made suggestions and contributions to this little book. Many pages could have been added, but the desire was to keep the volume small and handy. Although it would be impossible to name a lifetime of friendships, I must credit Edward Hewitt, my mentor of long ago; Eric Hallberg, a noteworthy French fly-casting expert; Charles Ritz, master of the Risle; my companions of the Houghton Club of Stockbridge, England; the O'Briens of County Kerry, Ireland; Philip Higgins of Oughterard; my friends of northern Wyoming and the Colorado waters, including Dorthe Cable of Cheyenne, Wyoming, Communications Chief of the Recreation Commission and Lloyd W. (Buck) Searle, Manager, Fish Division, Game and Fish Department, State of Colorado (retired); in northern New Mexico, the Vaughans of Chama Land and Cattle Company; Forbes Pennycook, an illustrious fisherman of the Pecos and San Juan river waters; Dr. Philip Shultz, whose enthusiasm and encouragement were essential; Gene Pacheco, whose assistance in making the illustrations was invaluable; and Paul Harbaugh of Denver, whose religion is fly fishing. My patient wife Barbara, who has, over the years, been most helpful and has withstood certain indignities incurred by a wandering husband who was always seeking new riffles and pools, also deserves my appreciation. Last, but not least, I gratefully acknowledge the help of Nathan Skallman, who at gunpoint made me finish the book.

Michel Pijoan
Corrales, New Mexico
1985

GAME FISH OF THE
ROCKY MOUNTAINS

INTRODUCTION

The Rocky Mountain range has many streams, rivers, and lakes, and most of them contain trout of various species and varieties, according the Rockies and their valleys a well-deserved reputation for excellent fishing. The Yellowstone, the Big Hole, the Firehole, and the Madison, to name only a few, bring anglers from all over our country and the world. In my own experience fishing in these waters, I discovered that many of these fishermen have been coming to our pleasant western clime year after year, delighting in cool nights and fast streams with their sporting fish.

The Rocky Mountains are the result not only of erosion but also of tremendous upheavals. This mountain range was created between the Eocene and Miocene times (sixteen million years ago) and developed isolated seas that eventually formed the plains of modern Colorado, the valleys behind Colorado Springs, and the extensive watershed and tributaries of the North Platte in Wyoming. It would appear that the high basin waters of western Montana and the Big Hole country of Yellowstone National Park were created as comparatively recently as the Pleistocene period (one million years ago).

It should be noted that Pleistocene glaciers occurred in cycles. In time, as the glaciers retreated northward with the warming of the climate, cold rivers formed behind the melting ice and depressions became lakes. Thus, the Pleistocene era was a period of remarkable geologic change as well as dramatic alterations in flora and fauna. The Rockies, like the earth itself, are still changing. Naturalist John Muir noted in the late nineteenth century that at Lone Pine Lake, "succeed-

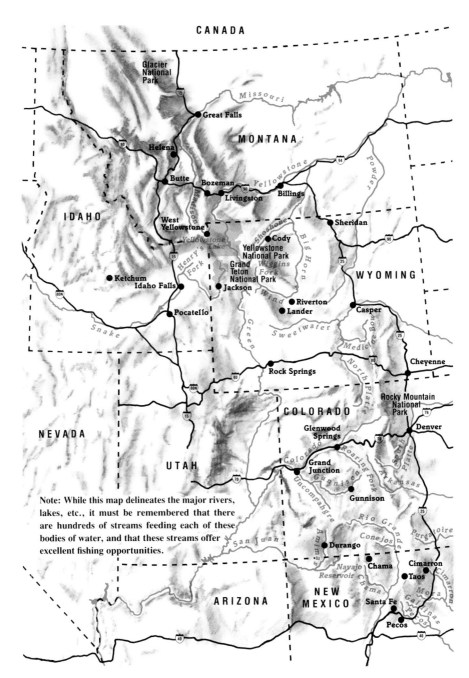

Note: While this map delineates the major rivers, lakes, etc., it must be remembered that there are hundreds of streams feeding each of these bodies of water, and that these streams offer excellent fishing opportunities.

General Area of American Rocky Mountain Fishing Waters

ing shocks, with rocks tumbling down, great boulders hurling themselves into the valley below, luminous from friction . . . the roar of the trembling mountains, [created] awful sound[s], equal to all other thunderstorms put together."

The ancestors of today's Rocky Mountain game fish entered the glacial melt and many were trapped in the headwaters of the Columbia River; later, they migrated throughout the Rocky Mountain watershed. The Cutthroat trout (in its many permutations) is an ancient species, as are other Charr and Salmon trout species. Three separate major strains of Cutthroats are distributed throughout the waters of Colorado and New Mexico: the so-called Colorado Cutthroat is distributed from the headwaters of the Green River in Wyoming to the foot of the Rockies in New Mexico; the rare Greenback Cutthroat, once prominent in east-slope rivers, is distributed in the Platte and Arkansas river systems, from Sweetwater in Wyoming to Purgatory in southern Colorado, the Pecos above Santa Fe, the Rio Puerco, and the Chama; the third subspecies occupies the Rio Grande. To my knowledge, there are at least seventeen subspecies or varieties, all with the red slash under their lower jaw. The Golden trout *(Salmo agua-bonito)* and its subspecies, also remnants of prehistoric fish strains, prefer the waters of very high altitudes, usually 10,000 feet above sea level. There, where the bitter winds blow, the Golden trout inhabit small high-country lakes and streams.

An enormous variety of fish have been transplanted in modern times as well. For example, in 1882 the Brown trout was imported into the United States from Germany; egg shipments continued and by 1889, the species had established itself in the rivers of Long Island. These particular fish, the original trout of European waters, were then transplanted to the Rocky Mountain fish habitat. Rainbow trout, an estuary fish with pronounced anadromous behavior (these fish have split personalities, so to speak; they can live in salt water but must breed in fresh water), were also imported into western waters during the period 1870 to 1895.

As new fishing practices developed and taxonomists became more discerning, many disclosures of "new" species were made, to the difficulty of ichthyologists. There are ongoing disputes even today among those whose lifework is the study of variations in fish life. In this handbook, I have endeavored to identify and discuss the most prominent of the Rocky Mountain game-fish types. Over a period of many years, I have often been asked about the game fish of the Rocky Mountains—how they live, how they migrate, when they spawn—and conceived that a handbook such as this one could make a contribution to those dedicated anglers who patiently endure the cold waters of Rocky Mountain fishing streams. It must be noted that some of the fish described in this handbook may not necessarily be considered game fish. Catfish, for instance, are frequently taken on trotlines and are usually not felt to rate the elegant title of "game fish";

however, as a two-pound catfish taken by chance on a single line can put up a fight worthy of the best game fish, it seems fitting to include them in this guidebook. Similarly, carp, bluegill, perch, and others are great sport for the novice or occasional fisherman. Thus, this little handbook must be read in the light of the occasion and the context of fishing as a sport, of an individual and his environment.

HOW A FISH FUNCTIONS

Fish are vertebrates: that is, they have a jointed backbone, which, with the rest of the skeleton, supports and strengthens the body. In the shark and skate families, this is composed of cartilage (gristle), but in the game fishes it is almost entirely true bone. The backbone consists of a series of hollow or cupshaped joints called vertebrae. These are connected by ligaments, the hollows being filled with a stiff jelly that acts as a kind of ball-and-socket gelatin. In this way, the backbone gains that great flexibility so characteristic of fish.

The ribs do not really create a rib cage, and there is no connecting breastbone (sternum). Actually, the ribs are within the muscle system of the fish, possibly adding a support to the musculature. The skull is formed of many bones that collectively provide for the protection of the brain and gills.

In the front of the fish are the pectoral fins, then the ventral fins, followed, in many fish, by an anal fin just in front of the tail. The number, size, position, and color of the fins, including the large dorsal fin on the back, constitute one of the easiest ways of identifying fish. Fish in the salmon family, for instance, have besides a dorsal fin, a small, fatty, extra dorsal fin called the adipose fin. Trout, which are Salmonoids, all have this small, extra fin. Some fish have no ventral fins, only pectoral fins. The number and variety are always characteristic of the species.

Weightless in water, fish use their fins for regulating direction, stabilizing, or making maneuvers. The most delicate flutter of a single fin can change a trout's position. The fins can be folded when speed is induced by the rapid back-and-forth motion of the caudal and anal fins. Maximum speeds can be obtained in this manner.

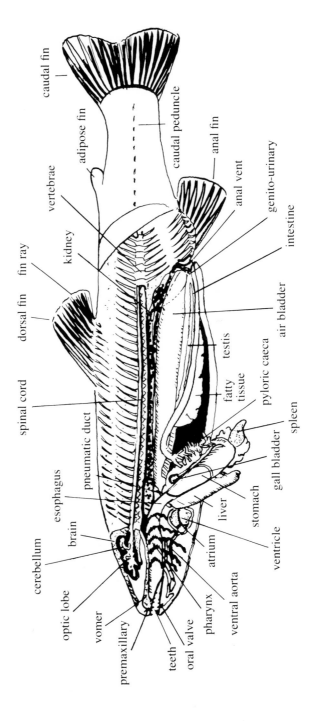

General Anatomy of Fish

caudal fin

adipose fin

caudal peduncle

anal fin

vertebrae

anal vent

genito-urinary

kidney

intestine

fin ray

dorsal fin

air bladder

testis

spinal cord

fatty
tissue

pyloric caeca

pneumatic duct

spleen

esophagus

gall bladder

brain

stomach

cerebellum

liver

ventricle

optic lobe

atrium

vomer

ventral aorta

premaxillary

pharynx

teeth

oral valve

6

The anal fin asserts its rhythm with a glide-and-stroke action, while the pectoral fins can be warped and extended, causing the fish to rise or descend at will; the movement of one fin can change its turn. This is true of the secondary role of the ventral fins, too. As well as helping to stabilize the fish in water, the pelvic fins help sustain the fish resting on the bottom.

The single dorsal and anal fins are used as vertical stabilizers (similar to the keel of a sailboat), inhibiting wobble and roll. The dorsal fin can be warped, compensating for instability. Furthermore, the paired fins are used as brakes. All fins are used when a fish jumps. A great deal can be written on the coordination of fin movements—what I have included is but a brief summary.*

Fish differ from most terrestrial animals in that the latter undergo changes on their outer surface that keep them clear of parasites. Thus, when snakes slough their skins and birds moult, the protective layers are constantly renewed. In the case of fish, the skin and scales are permanent; the scales are never shed. The layer of slime thus provides an additional measure of protection. Parasites or fungus spores that attach themselves to the fish are engulfed in the slime and thereby inhibited in development. It is only when the solid protection of the scales is missing that infections take over. Wounded fish that have lost scales become easy prey for fungus, which will take over the wounded area. (For this reason anglers need to take great care in handling a fish that is to be returned to water.)

The trout's scales are so small as to be hardly visible. They exist under the skin, in a fold covered by a membrane. As a fish grows, its scales expand and form a protective covering. The scales actually increase in size to fit the fish; the number, however, remains constant. The scales develop by successive accretions, or rings. If conditions are good, particularly in the summer, growth is rapid and the rings in the scales become more widely spaced. The age of a fish can be determined by counting these rings, much as the age of a tree can be determined by counting its rings. The scales are considered a part of the skin of the fish. In addition to the scales, the skin is protected by a layer of slime or mucous.

Anatomically, trout and other fish have organs similar to those of the higher animals, but the organs are arranged in a way that makes them difficult to recognize. The heart and the liver with its gall sac are set close together in the neck section of the body, in what might be called the upper thorax. The kidney, which lies along the backbone, is the heavy streak of blood the angler takes out with his thumbnail when cleaning a fish. The stomach is large and the intestine small; a considerable absorption of nutrients occurs, therefore, in the stomach.

The fish's mouth contains numerous taste buds that determine the selection

---

*From notes taken by the author of his observations of trout in the aquariums of the Ghost Ranch Museum in Abiquiu, New Mexico. At that time, he was on the Board of Directors of the Living Museum.

and acceptance of food. Many fish, unless they are struck and hooked at once, will spit out artificial lures. Most fish have teeth and in fact it is the arrangement of teeth that indicates to which genus the fish belongs. If a trout has a single or double row of teeth on the front and rear of the vomer bone (located in the front part of the roof of the mouth), the trout is of the genus *Salmo* (Brown trout, for example). If, on the other hand, the teeth exist as a single patch at the rear of the bone, one has a charr trout of the genus *Salvelinus* (Brook trout, for example). In general, if food particles are not too large they will be swallowed whole, but should they be too large to pass through the pharynx, the teeth play a part in breaking the particles down to an appropriate size.

Food taken by the fish enters through the mouth (buccal cavity) and passes through the throat (pharynx) into the esophagus, which extends from the throat to the stomach. The pharynx is quite muscular and crushes the food as it passes down to the stomach. By means of strong contractions, the stomach grinds the food further; in addition to being a tough muscular pouch, the stomach is also a very complex organ which produces chemicals for the digestion of food. It contains layers of cells that secrete hydrochloric acid and digestive enzymes that convert food into nutrients assimilated by the fish. The final products of digestion are absorbed by the many small projections that are present around the base of the stomach and intestines. The liver secretes bile into the gall bladder, which in turn empties into the lower intestine. Special enzymes are also secreted by the pancreas. The entire process of digestion is anything but simple.

The importance of the liver is not to be underestimated. Aside from its function in bile production and hormone regulation, it acts as a warehouse for the storage of proteins, fats, and certain starches and sugars. It is also rich in vitamins. During winter months, the liver plays an important role in the survival of fish. When the water temperature drops, there is a slowing up of activity and a decrease in appetite; once frost, ice, and cold weather take over, the liver becomes the main source of nutrition in supporting the life of the fish.

In place of aerating lungs, fish have gills, comprised of plates that contain many small vessels (capillaries). These gills absorb dissolved oxygen in water, and in turn liberate carbon dioxide. Thus, the exchange of gases takes place through membranes that have surface contact directly with the water.

The thyroid is located at the base of the mouth. If iodine is lacking, the thyroid becomes enlarged and can easily be felt. Pituitary, adrenal, and pancreatic glands are also present. These control the fish's growth, maturation, and certain responses to stimuli.

The swim bladder, which fills with nitrogen, is an organ unique to fish. Since nitrogen gas is much lighter than water, the bladder stabilizes the position of the fish and gives the fish the buoyancy needed for maintaining and adjusting its level in water. The bladder fills by the removal of almost pure nitrogen from the circulating blood. When there are changes in barometric pressure, the swim bladder responds. With increased barometric pressure the gas is compressed, and conversely, with a decrease in pressure, the gas expands. If there is considerable expansion of the bladder, creating pressure on the stomach and adjacent organs, the trout will take less food.

During a heavy fall in the barometer, I have observed that trout become agitated, move about in an excited way, and refuse the flies cast to them. On numerous occasions, I have also noticed that quick changes of the barometer in either direction have a decided influence on the feeding activity of fish.* When these rapid changes occur, fish will often stop feeding. But there are exceptions to the rule. Sometimes at high altitudes during a storm they will take food eagerly; a sufficient cloud cover may bring about a sudden rise of fish. Often, at a storm's peak, when the angler stands in shadows and feels diminished by the weather, the fish respond by taking flies previously rejected.

A great deal has been written about the eyes and vision of fish. The subject is obviously of importance because it is related to the ability of fish to seek food, whether real or artificial. The eyes not only see but receive light and color stimuli. For this reason the coloring of the body responds to variations in environment. When, for example, a trout is blind in one eye, that side of the body may become somewhat dark, and when blind in both eyes, the trout may become quite dark in color. I recall fishing a pond above the Chama waterfalls, in New Mexico. The large fish there failed to take any kind of lure. Several of these large fish were later caught by hand and were found to have growths over their eyes that rendered the cornea fairly opaque. These trout had apparently developed the disease late in life or they would not have grown to such size. I doubt that they would have survived much longer, because they could not see well enough to feed. The normal trout's hue will change according to the prevailing color of the stream bottom; such changes will take place rapidly.

The eye of the fish is not like the human eye: the fish eye is almost spherical and cannot be made to focus by changing the shape of the lens, as with mammalian eyes. The muscles act by drawing the fixed-sized lens either closer to or farther from the retina, much as we do in focusing a camera. Like the fish's eye, the lens in a camera remains a fixed structure, and focusing is achieved by moving closer to or farther away from the photographic film or plate. The surface of a fish's retina has movable rods and cones, and these are drawn in front of one another to expose a maximum number of rods for low-light vision. The fish's eye has a very large pupil, and it is assumed because of this that it has great light-gathering power. Trout can see rather well in dusky to dark conditions.

---

*Many of us have considerable faith in our barometers: if low pressure is present with the barometer falling, it usually means poor fishing, whereas a rising barometer indicates favorable fishing conditions. At higher altitudes the rules are often broken, and a fisherman should be guided, but not regulated, by his instruments. Judgement and experience are better.

Many studies have been performed to determine the range of vision in trout. As a fisherman approaches a stream and is able to see trout, it becomes immediately apparent that the trout, in turn, often see him, especially if the fisherman is moving about. The trout will be seen darting upstream in all directions to hide from what appears to them to be a large moving object. If the fisherman is careful, moves slowly, or hides behind boulders or bushes, he can approach the wary trout and make his cast.

Studies reveal that a fish can see either the surface or out of the water at an angle of about forty-eight degrees. It is apparent that if the fish turns in all directions, the window of vision will become circular. Experiments bear this out. The angle from the bottom plane to the vertical axis, on the other hand, is about forty-one degrees. Fishermen have known for some time that in certain conditions it is best not to cast directly over the fish, but rather upstream, allowing the current to bring the fly into the trout's window of vision.

Of course, this window of vision is not always the same but increases in diameter with the depth of the water over the fish. In shallow water, the window will be smaller; in deeper water, the window is larger. In shallow water, the fly must come close to the trout in order to be taken: in deeper water the fly or lure can be cast some distance away from the fish.

Although we cannot know with certainty just what the fish sees, we must assume that it is pretty much what we see. Many photographs and studies have been made under water, and it is presumed that images of simple surface objects, either blurred or radiant to us, must appear somewhat the same to fish. It is possible, however, and highly probable, that trout can see better underwater than we do. Their vision is acute, and under certain conditions, the trout are easily frightened by a leader of .004 inch diameter. They can see the smallest gnats.

When a fly or other object breaks the surface of the water, a progression of little waves form, creating a series of flashes. Bright light creates a mirror effect on still water. This is alarming and will often frighten fish. At other times, it acts as a stimulus that will attract curious fish. It is evident that if a fly is floating high on the water, the fish will see only those portions of the fly that break through the surface.

Are fish colorblind? It has been believed that they react to color in the same way that colorblind people do. However, the burden of evidence favors the view that fish see most of the colors and shades of colors well enough to respond to degrees of brightness and shades of ultraviolet light. Furthermore, they apparently recognize shapes of objects. Fish have been trained to distinguish circles from squares and ovals. The fishermen must not only find the right color and pattern of fly, but the proper size, as well.

Professor Karl van Fritsch at the University of Munich investigated the hearing of fish. He used a high-pitched whistle, which he followed with a feeding period. After fifteen or twenty such feedings, when the conditioned reaction was obtained, he used the whistle alone and the fish responded by going to their feeding place. The sound could be heard, and was responded to, from a distance of some two hundred feet from the aquarium. They appear to hear the same low and high intensities that we do. The vestibular organs in the ear of the fish help to regulate balance.

Edward R. Hewitt made repeated observations on salmon. When he approached a pond where he believed Atlantic salmon were present, he would clap his hands loudly; he found that many of them would disclose themselves by leaping into the air. It has been known that trout will sometimes stop rising when conversations take place near still waters. Again, we must adhere to Izaak Walton's advice, "Study to be quiet."

All fish have organs of smell. They have two small holes, clearly visible on the upper jaw, and water runs through these holes by small pumplike mechanisms. Odor diffuses slowly in water, but when water is in motion, odors will pass quickly to a fish. When meat is thrown in a stream, trout may come rapidly to the source from which the meat has been thrown.

They taste with organ buds, which are distributed throughout the mouth, tongue, and lip margins. Trout show preferences for different insects at different times. They are particularly fond of May flies because of their high fat content. At other times, they will ignore all insects except flying ants, which have a high acid content. All anglers are familiar with the way Brook trout will spit out the fly before it is taken.

Another sense organ of the fish is the so-called acousti-colateral (lateral line) system. This organ can usually be identified by a deeply colored line extending from behind the gill plate, along the mid-portion of the fish, to its tail. In some fish, it is highly colored; in others, it assumes a dark hue. This line is not just a band of color but contains a delicate mechanism. There is within it a remarkable nerve supply with little hillocks containing small, sensitive hairs. It has been proven quite conclusively that this line on the side of a fish registers vibrations as well as changes in water currents. For example, fish will keep their station in a stream for long periods of time by swimming against the current just fast enough to compensate for the water's speed. Any change in current or vibration will be registered through this lateral line. As the impulses are transmitted to the brain, the fish will respond promptly. In darkness, this control is essential. The fish senses the presence of rocks and other structures by the changing current, or water pressure, as detected by the lateral line. As a result, the lateral line has often been called the distant-touch system. It has been noted that if the lateral line is severed, fish will often have collisions with the walls of an aquarium. There is also some evidence to support the opinion that the lateral line may record temperature changes.

The reproductive organs lie in the abdominal cavity near the swim bladder and below the kidney. Both the eggs in the hen fish and the milt (sperm and sperm fluid) in the male fish are expelled through the anal vent (cloaca), and during spawning, the eggs occupy much of the space in the female's abdomen. Significantly, hen fish are rarely found without eggs present in the abdomen. Shortly after the spawning event, new eggs begin to form; these will remain and mature until the following spawning season.

Late autumn, when the intensity of illumination decreases and water temperatures become cooler, is the time when Brook trout spawn. Spawning may be artificially induced in captive Brook trout by means of manipulating the light intensity (a gradual decrease) and chilling the water of the aquarium. Fertilization of the eggs takes place externally. A small, but sexually mature, male trout may often fertilize the eggs of a much larger female. Under ideal conditions, fish sperm retain vigor for some time, and for artificial breeding purposes may be stored for many hours. The sperm are motionless in the spermatic fluid, but once in contact with water, they become intensely active and survive for only a few minutes. The eggs of the hen fish secrete a substance, fertilizin, that attracts sperm. The sperm also secrete substances, gynogamones, that hold them to the eggs and alter the egg membrane, allowing the sperm to penetrate. Water continues to enter the egg after it is fertilized, and hardening takes place within twenty-four hours.

There are variations in the way fish spawn. In general, the female chooses the location for the nest (redd) in the end of a shallow pool. She then hollows a pit in the gravel by turning on her side and sweeping the gravel from side to side with her tail. She returns many times to the same spot to repeat this action, making the nest deeper each time. Meanwhile, the male fish lingers to one side and drives away other males. Then he swims over the female, in general courtship behavior, rubbing his nose and head against her body. The completed nest is a depression in the sand or gravel, about four to five inches deep, and from eight to twelve inches in diameter. It is usually shorter than a fish's length, so that the hen fish must curve her body to enter it.

When the female trout appears ready to lay her eggs and is lying almost sideways in the nest, she is joined by the male, who assumes a similar position. They become rigid and eggs and milt are expelled into the pit. Male and female fish quiver slightly during the spawning act.

Immediately after spawning is completed, both fish leave the nest. In less than a minute, the female will return to the nest and start to cover the eggs with gravel. It usually takes nearly an hour to cover the eggs. Once this is accomplished, the female moves away and starts work on another pit, where she will deposit more eggs. The male stays nearby and guards the nest against intruders. This process may go on intermittently for about one week.

If the eggs are carefully laid and properly covered with gravel, they will be protected from light and natural enemies. Water circulates through the gravel, bringing oxygen to the egg surfaces. After approximately fifty days, depending upon water temperature and variety of trout, the alevins (newly hatched offspring, with yolk sacs still attached) cling to the gravel nest until the yolk is fully absorbed. Once the yolk has been completely used, the young fish make their way slowly up from the gravel beds and start life on their own, in open water.

Environmental conditions

The production of fish in streams will vary with the character of the water, the kind of bottom, the vegetation, the degree of aeration, and the nutrients available. Studies have shown considerable variation in the number of fish per acre of water; in poor streams, where conditions are not good, there may be a yield of as little as six pounds per acre. Narrow, deeper streams produce far more fish than shallow, wide streams—there is more bank present in the deeper streams and usually more food. Furthermore, as a stream warms, cooler temperatures will occur in the deeper water. However, a shallow stream that is wide and has fast water and pools can be equally good for the growth of trout.

The growth of trout in streams is generally greater than in lakes, which have acid waters low in lime salts and can yield a small number of fish. Water vegetation is essential and without it, trout do poorly. Vegetation creates an excellent environment for aquatic crustaceans and other small animals. Furthermore, the vegetation liberates oxygen into the water and absorbs carbon dioxide. In places where vegetation is removed to improve fishing for anglers using spinning lures, the fish will also do poorly.

All fish require oxygen for survival. They get this essential gas from the water, where it has been either synthesized by plants or is present as a result of aeration (fresh air introduced into water, or naturally mixing near the surface). Placing boulders in creeks and rivers and creating small dams, which in turn create small waterfalls, greatly increases aeration. This is particularly significant when accomplished in the inlets of lakes or ponds. The more water that is churned at an inlet to a lake, the more free oxygen there will be. This, in turn, will result in a greater rate of growth for the fish.

Trout do best when the free oxygen exceeds six parts per million, and will die if it is two and one-half parts (or less) per million. The oxygen fish utilize is not dissolved from water (H_2O), but is free oxygen (O_2) that comes from plants through photosynthesis or through aeration. A high oxygen content is not injurious to trout. In fact, if the oxygen content of the water is four parts per million, the trout will move toward the higher oxygen content. Hewitt observed that in a pool of twenty square feet, with a water flow of sixty gallons per minute and with five hundred pounds of trout in residence, the oxygen was reduced from eight parts per million to six parts per million. He found that water falling just a foot over a board weir added a very necessary one part of oxygen per million, and that if the weir was irregular and saw-toothed, then two parts of oxygen were added.

Aside from the oxygenation of water, the temperature of the water will have a determining influence on the survival of trout. Trout will live at 32°F, but in waters this cold, their metabolic processes will be considerably slowed up: very little food will be required, and weight loss may take place. Observations of trout living in very cold environments disclosed by experiment that food intake often remained in the stomach for as long as two weeks. At 42°, digestion is completed in about five days; at 52°, the same food is digested in about twenty-four hours; and at 62°, in about twelve hours. Hewitt's experiments determined that the most efficient digestion for Rainbow trout takes place at about 65° F. Above 70°, they will slack off and fail to eat very much. However, these situations may be affected by the food the fish already have in their stomach. If the stomach is full, temperature will be a definite factor in determining the further intake of food.

The winter season is the most destructive time for fish and winter kill can be significant if temperatures drop severely. Trout almost cease to feed at 32°, and furthermore, water under ice can have little or no current, and vital aeration is therefore reduced. Vegetation, even though it is dormant, may act as a buffer. For this reason, trout tend to go downstream in search of more favorable conditions. In the spring and early summer, many streams yield striking fish in the morning, but in the afternoon when the run upstream takes place, the trout will not respond because the water may be too cold. Later, the reverse may be true: when the snows have thawed, the water may warm, creating ideal conditions in the afternoon.

The creation of good deep holes in streams will allow favorable habitats for resting fish during the winter. Holes dug a mile or less apart in small streams will ensure the survival of many trout. Such holes have been introduced in many of the famous streams of the East; in the West, however, accommodations for wintering fish have not been established.

In spring and summer when the weather has been hot and a heavy rain has occurred, the trout will become hungry and start feeding if the water has not been muddied. Rain also washes food into streams, and a rise in the water level will usually excite fish into feeding. A long period of hot weather without wind will put the fish down, causing poor fishing. In ponds, when it has been hot and windless, there will be fewer waves to aerate the water.*

Trout in lakes and ponds may be in shallow water early in the season for feeding purposes because of the somewhat warmer water. I have often waded out into lakes in late spring and cast toward shore, having considerable success in taking large fish this way. In mid-summer when the weather is warm, fishermen will often use a thermometer to find the cooler waters. When wading, one can note the changes in water temperature by the sensation of coldness against the

---

*Many anglers believe that fishing is good just before an approaching storm, particularly if a wind is present. Ordinarily, cobwebs and dew on the grass indicate a fair fishing day (perhaps).

boot. If the day has been very warm, the fishing will be best during the early morning or at dusk, after the water has been cooled by the night air. The lake or pond is likely to be deserted and privacy of fishing will be assured. Water that seemed dead and cleared of fish during the day will become dimpled by rising fish during these times.

Appetites of fish vary according to size, age, and environmental conditions, such as water temperature and crowding. Young fish (fry) often eat until they bulge, and then will act more or less indifferent to food for a period of time. Mature fish may be voracious eaters at times, but in general, their appetite is far less than that of growing fish; they never eat to excess or distort their streamlined shapes. Some fish are vegetarians, others are meat eaters, and some eat both types of food. Most fish can alter their diets if necessity dictates.

Under natural conditions, variations in feeding habits occur during the spawning cycle. Food consumption drops off at least sixty percent in the few weeks before spawning, and during the actual spawning phase, little or no food is found in the stomachs. Accumulation and increase in fat storage and liver nutrients take place prior to the full maturity of the reproductive organs.

In an aquarium, trout adjust poorly to dietary changes. In hatcheries, the problem can be serious but has been solved by using liver and beef lights (lungs), which the trout seem to like and thrive upon. Recently, dried-food diets have been introduced that contain all the factors necessary for growth.

Lime salts appear to be important for the growth of trout, and it has been proven that water high in lime salts produce the largest fish. Thus, 2.8 to 14 parts per million of lime (as calcium oxide) gives poor biological activity, whereas 50 to 140 parts per million produce the highest fish growth and yield. Studies in the Catskill streams, where 8 to 10 parts per million of lime salts are present, showed that these conditions were poor for trout growth.

Contrary to the opinions of some, trout will grow throughout their lives if proper conditions exist. At the Bellefort Hatchery in Pennsylvania, a trout was observed for some fifteen years. Well along in life in 1942, the fish weighed twenty-three pounds, had a length of thirty-two and one-half inches, and a depth of ten inches. This Brown trout was fifteen years old when it died, and had been kept under careful observation in a concrete pool throughout its life. At its death in 1946, its length was thirty-five inches, its depth ten inches, and it weighed twenty-seven pounds.

In poor environmental conditions, trout called "snakers" have been taken that have huge heads and slim bodies, no more than six to eight inches in length. These snakers had poor nutritional conditions, and had probably attained their full growth. Interestingly, eggs from these fish will grow normally and will carry no lingering effects to the offspring. If "snake" trout occur in streams or ponds where a deficiency of minerals or food is present, measures must be taken if fishing is to be improved.

When hatchery fingerlings are introduced in ponds, they may fail to adapt at first to the diet of plankton and other small creatures because they were reared under artificial conditions with hatchery food. It is often essential to supplement their diets with other foods, for it may take these fish weeks or months to build themselves up on the new environmental diet.

SALMON FAMILY

Whitefish, grayling, trout, and salmon are all members of the salmon family, Salmonidae. Within this family, taxonomists recognize two principal groups: the trout, belonging to the genus *Salmo,* and the charr, belonging to the genus *Salvelinus.* Thus, while both the Rainbow trout and the Brook trout are of the same family, taxonomists recognize these fish as salmon trout and charr trout, respectively.

Charrs have no teeth upon the front of the bone in the roof of the mouth, whereas salmon trout do. The word "charr" is derived from the Gaelic "cear," meaning red or blood-colored.* The word is therefore applicable to the male Brook trout at spawning time when its belly has a brilliant red color. Charrs can behave like salmon in that some species live in the sea and ascend the rivers to spawn. Salmon and trout are very closely related.

Trout are the predominant game fish of the Rocky Mountains. Although there are a number of other worthy game fish, trout are the best known and the most eagerly sought after. There are four basic types in the Rocky Mountain region: the Cutthroat, the Rainbow, the Brown, and the Brook. At times one of these may be easier to catch than the others. The Brown trout seem to have a higher tolerance for warmer waters and will survive where conditions are unsuitable for other trout. Removal of trees and vegetation may increase the temperature of streams, and the Brook trout, requiring much colder water than others, may

---

*In the Arctic, where charr trout live in great profusion, one cannot but feel that these fish belong to receding glacial periods. The Arctic charr is the major species of fish found south of the Arctic Circle.

become hard to find. Rainbow and Cutthroat trout appear to adapt most easily to the environmental conditions of the higher Rocky Mountain waters.

SALMON TROUT
(SALMO)

RAINBOW TROUT *(SALMO GAIRDNERII)*

The Rainbow trout, once native to the Pacific coast from southern California to Alaska, has since been introduced to most waters across the continent. It is a fine game fish and offers great challenge to most anglers. Among its characteristics is its ability to survive in generally warmer water than the Brook trout, but only if the water is well aerated. The Rainbow feeds upon insects, crustaceans, worms, and smaller fishes. These salmon trout are one of the most muscular and resourceful of fishes, and are held in high regard as a hardy fish by most fishermen. The Rainbow appears to be more resistant to disease than other trout. The great ferocity that they display in colder, faster water becomes quiescent in ponds and still waters.

The Rainbow, like all other trout, is extremely variable in color, spot formation, and body form. The confusion in nomenclature can become exasperating. About thirty years ago, some fifteen separate species of Rainbow were described, including the Steelhead, a large Rainbow migrating between the sea and fresh water, and the Kamloops, an inland form of Rainbow growing to a large size. Today, taxonomists recognize one species of Rainbow trout and five subspecies. Rainbow trout are the most migratory of all.

In cold lakes, with plenty of food, these fish grow to a remarkable size, while in waters with a sparse food supply, growth is negligible for several years. This fish was imported to the British Isles not only as a hefty sporting fish, but because it grew much more quickly than any native British trout. In England, the Houghton Club breeds Rainbows of huge size for purposes of stocking streams (Test and Itchen).

Physical characteristics

Unlike the Cutthroats, the Rainbows do not have the characteristic reddish or yellowish streak beneath the lower jaw. The Rainbow differs also in having a shorter upper jaw. Occasionally, some streaking may occur, which may be the result of interbreeding with Cutthroat. The general color of the trout is silver, with a soft-green or light-blue back. The gill covers are of a somewhat rosy hue, and have light and dark spots that are often barely visible on the sides.

The scales of the Rocky Mountain Rainbow are easily visible and are more apparent than those of other trout. The lower fins are yellowish, and the adipose

Rainbow Trout (*Salmo gairdnerii*)

fin has a black margin in young fish, whereas it is spotted in the older or larger individuals. Body, dorsal, adipose, and caudal fins all have numerous dark spots. The other fins may be of a rather light, white color, or somewhat pink. Most Rainbows have a generalized silver color with hues of pink and lavender on the sides of the lateral line.

The Rainbow has a typical trout shape. Immature fish possess the usual parr marks (marks found on fish that are at the intermediate stage between alevin and adult). Often a pink or lavender band exists as a blush from gill cover to tail. This coloring reminds many anglers with vivid imaginations of an actual rainbow. There are twelve rays in the anal fin (not to be confused with the caudal fin) in the Rainbow and Steelhead, an easy count to distinguish this trout.

Spawning

The typical, or coast range, trout will seek the colder upstream waters to spawn. In contrast to the Brook trout, the Rainbows spawn in the spring on rising temperatures, rather than in the autumn on falling ones. In hatcheries, spawning can be achieved in all seasons. In the wilds, the location, altitude, and temperature make spring spawning a once-a-year adventure. The general courtship of the male and the female fish, as well as egg laying and spawning, is the same as that of the Brook trout. In many instances, however, two male fish will care for and protect a single female.

Female Rainbows, when they are ready to spawn, become active workers in preparing the nests or redds, scooping up gravel with their bodies, making adequate depressions for the eggs. These depressions or beds may often equal the whole lengths of their bodies.

The cockfish stands by, ready to fight off intruders. Completing their redds, the hen fish drop back into the depression and are joined by the male. Both fish writhe together, the male often stroking the female along the caudal peduncle. A shuddering motion takes place, and suddenly both eggs and milt are simultaneously extruded. New eggs tumble into the current and many are promptly consumed by other fish. The remaining eggs are carefully covered with gravel or small stones.

The stamina of these fish is an unforgettable sight as the female plies her way upstream to start a second redd and repeat the egg-laying and mating drama. Such spawning rites have been known to continue for several days, up to a week. After these exhausting performances, both female and male appear fully spent. These fish are then called kelts, and will drift downstream into deep waters, recovering their strength in a quiet, deep pool. It can take weeks of feeding on small fish, crustaceans, and mollusks before their strength is totally restored.

Lake Rainbows migrate upstream to spawn. Small females produce some four hundred to eight hundred eggs, while a four-pound hen fish will yield as many as twenty-five hundred to three thousand eggs. Incubation is about thirty days at 50°F. The alevin, those that avoid being eaten by other fish or their parents, will remain hidden in water weeds for varying lengths of time. Once the yolk sacs are absorbed, some of these fish will return eventually to the lake. Others will remain in the stream for months, or even years. The young feed on immature aquatic insects and small crustaceans, while mature fish consume enormous quantities of nymphs, other insect larvae, crustaceans, and small fish.

At Lake Pend Oreille, Idaho, Rainbows (Kamloops) grow to an enormous size, feeding on land-locked Kokanee salmon. Record catches of fifteen to twenty-pound fish are not uncommon. There was a Rainbow taken at Lake Pend Oreille that weighed thirty-seven pounds.

The Rainbow is the subject of much experimental work, particularly at the School of Fisheries, University of Oregon. One experiment there produced large numbers of fertile eggs yielding quantities of strong, healthy, climate-adjusted fingerlings for use in streams and lakes. Such selective breeding has produced significant results: from one to two thousand eggs in four-year-old spawners in 1932, to over five thousand eggs in three-year-olds in 1955. Such is the drive to increase Rainbows for planting around the world. In Rocky Mountain streams, and particularly in the Yellowstone waters, Rainbows are prevalent, even though some streams have large Cutthroat populations. In the Jackson Hole area, for example, Brown trout are sought, but Rainbow or Cutthroat are usually taken.

STEELHEAD TROUT
(*SALMO GAIRDNERII:* ANADROMOUS FORM)

Rainbow trout *(Salmo gairdnerii),* as have been previously discussed, are quite at home in mountain lakes and streams; they have no knowledge of the sea. The old saying that "you won't miss what you don't know," could, if fancy permits, apply to the large numbers of Rainbows in our Rocky Mountains. However, on occasion an anadromous Rainbow (an infrequent visitor), ascending a river to spawn, can be taken in waters on the edge of the Rockies in Oregon and Idaho; this form of Rainbow is called a Steelhead and is large and somewhat torpedo-shaped. They have been known to migrate as far as Lewiston, and sometimes even further into the mountain ranges. The Steelhead rears in fast, snow-melt-fed streams. Being anadromous, after feeding and growing to huge size in the sea, they migrate upstream for the purpose of spawning; afterward, they return downstream to recover in the salt water of the ocean.

The Steelhead, when hooked, offers stern resistance to capture; rated as one of the most exciting fish to land, their weight varies from ten to twenty-five pounds.

Spawning

Late autumn or winter-run Steelhead are sexually mature. The process of spawning is quite similar to that of the Rainbow, but is less intensive. Six or seven redds are usually required, the eggs being covered by the female. Some nests seem unnecessarily large—they can be as much as four to six feet long, and two to three feet wide, in about six inches of water.

A twenty-inch hen fish may produce from two thousand to three thousand eggs, whereas a thirty-inch fish of this species can produce ten thousand eggs. The young Steelhead may spend several years in fresh water, but sixty percent of the six-to-seven inch parr trout will head for the sea.

Steelhead return to fresh water as mature adults after being out to sea from four to seven years. It is of interest to note that spawning Steelhead will return to their parent stream, and, like the salmon, will have no appetite during the spawning season. In salt water, exhausted fish and the smaller Steelheads feed vigorously upon marine invertebrates and crustaceans. The larger fish prefer other, smaller fish for their diet. An old guide, observing this behavior among the Steelhead trout, once said to me, "Everybody seems to be eating everybody else."

GILA TROUT *(SALMO GILAE)*

This trout, one of the Rainbow varieties, is not a large species. It has a restricted range in a few of the headwaters of the Gila and San Francisco rivers in the mountains of southwestern New Mexico. Regardless of arguments about nomenclature, the American Fisheries Society lists the Gila trout as a distinct species, in some danger of extinction. It is not generally considered to be a Rocky Mountain fish.

The distinctive feature of the Gila trout is abundant spotting, particularly on the dorsal and caudal fins. The black spots are small and placed irregularly. There are more than six spots on the adipose fin. In the folds below the jaw are yellow-to-pink markings. The upper jaw is relatively long and extends beyond the rear of the eye. Gilas are a small fish when mature, from ten to fourteen inches in length at the largest.

There is some evidence that these trout were part of the Glacial Age. They appear, indeed, to be a remnant of an ancient fish.

BROWN TROUT *(SALMO TRUTTA,* ALIAS *FARIO)*

The Brown, or German, trout was first planted in our streams about 1883. When deforestation occurred in many areas and the water became unsuited or too warm for Brook trout, the Brown trout took over. This trout, although introduced from European waters, has made itself quite comfortable in our western waters.

The Brown trout grows rapidly if food is available, and, in fact, they are often incriminated as a fish that likes to eat other fish. This seems to be true, as they have a known appetite for minnows.

Brown Trout (*Salmo trutta*)

Brown trout are to be respected as one of the finest fighting game fish. There are two strains of Brown trout: one from Scottish waters, called the Loch Leven trout, and the other from Germany, called the Von Behr trout. It is impossible to distinguish one from the other when interbreeding has occurred.

A gentleman named Von Behr apparently exported the latter hardy trout to the United States. *Salmo trutta,* also called *Salmo fario,* was a delicacy to both the Romans, who built fish ponds to propagate these fish, and the ancient monks, who feasted upon them. The delicate flavor was enjoyed by all. In 1653, Izaak Walton referred to Brown trout as "the Trout," as did Dame Juliana Berners, Prioress of Sopwell, in 1486. The Brown trout now occupies a prominant position in forty-two states and most of Canada. The fish is more tolerant to temperature and environmental changes and is adaptable to conditions unsuited to charr or other trouts.

Brown trout have been known to rise viciously to the surface for most moving objects. They have even been known to rise at swallows skimming over the surface of the water. Dissection of the stomachs of these fish has revealed an astonishing variety of diet: mayflies, worms, mollusks, crayfish, freshwater shrimp, and other small fish. Larger Browns will consume frogs, mice, and small birds.

Physical characteristics

The Brown trout has more scales than either the Brook trout or the Rainbow. Their sides have a few red spots, but the predominant spotting of the body is a dark brown with black spots. The adipose fin (the fin between the dorsal and tail fins) is usually, but not always, marked with an orange-brown. The color of the body is a greenish-brown or an olive tinge that fades to yellow or white at the belly. The belly fins are of a somewhat yellow color. The Cutthroat trout is often mistaken for a Brown because of the color similarities.

The Brown trout, often called the Brownie, feeds actively on the surface. The larger Browns do most of their feeding at night or at dusk. They may hide under low-cut banks or beneath overhanging branches, usually preferring lively water with cover. But all rules can be broken, and Browns have often been taken in open water.

The Brownie is a strong and stubborn fighter, and easily grows to twenty inches in length. The larger fish are, in the main, flesh eaters, preying on smaller fish. Brown trout have a double row of teeth that runs down the central bone (vomer). Their tail is somewhat square, and there may be reddish or orange stripes on its edges.

Spawning

Spawning occurs from October to February, the eggs being laid in nests or redds in the gravel of a stream bottom. Depending on the size of the female, the eggs deposited vary from six hundred to six thousand per female. At water temperatures of about 50°F, hatching takes place in about fifty days.

These fish may crossbreed with the Brook trout, the progeny often marked like zebras. The name Zebra trout has been given to such offspring. The latter are barren; crossing salmon trout with charr trout always results in mule fish that are unable to reproduce.

The Brown trout's breeding habits are similar to those of the Brook trout, but it does not require lower water temperatures, nor does it need the aeration demanded by the Brook trout. Brown trout reproduce well, are hardy, sustain themselves through many different conditions (both with regard to weather and water), and are an admirable game fish.

CUTTHROAT TROUT *(SALMO CLARKII)*

The typical American Cutthroat is often referred to as the native trout. It ranges in coastal streams from Puget Sound to the Elk River of Humbolt County, California, and its varieties are found in the headwaters and tributaries of the Rio Grande, as well as in the Utah Basin. Its feeding habits are similar to those of the Rainbow. The Rio Grande Cutthroat *(Salmo clarkii spilurus)* is the most familiar to anglers in New Mexico.

Most Cutthroats in the Rocky Mountain region run eight to fourteen inches, although larger ones have been taken. The Rio Grande waters, from Taos to Alcalde, New Mexico, were once prime Cutthroat territory, where twenty-inch and three-pound fish were not uncommon. This water had a high reputation with fishermen from all over the world. At present, it is doubtful that any Cutthroat exist there. The fish have been replaced by thousands of coarse fish* and hatchery fish. Live minnows used as bait and then turned loose have usurped the food supply and have consumed the eggs of the Cutthroat. (Until live minnow bait is prohibited, this is likely to happen in most trout waters.)

The Cutthroat inhabits many different waters and has been hybridized to produce various genetic compositions, strains, and color schemes. In 1935, eleven subspecies of Cutthroat were reported. Oliver Cope, a Fishery Research Biologist, produced a listing of seventy common or vernacular names for the Cutthroat trout. So anglers, beware: there is the Alaska Cutthroat, the Black-speckled trout, the Colorado Cutthroat, the Greenback Cutthroat, the Lake Tahoe trout, the Platte Cutthroat, the Snake River Cutthroat, the Yellowstone trout, trouts of various Indian names, and a multitude of others.

---

*The term "coarse fish" resists specific definition. It is a name given generally to fish that take food away from trout and other sporting game fish. The minnow is a classic example. I have seen fishermen at quitting time dump large buckets of minnows in the stream. In turn, the fish propagate and grow to a large size.

Physical characteristics

The chief characteristic of the Cutthroat, the one from which its name is derived, is the distinct and well-defined red or orange streak in the folds beneath the lower jaw and in the streak appearing next to the gill cover and extending to beneath the jaw. The upper jaw of the adult fish is long, usually half as long as the head, and extends behind the seat of the eye. It is a handsome fish, liberally spattered with black and bright spots that extend to the tail and fins. It may have a somewhat rosy stripe on its sides, similar to that of the Rainbow.

The body of the Cutthroat is usually four times longer than its depth. The teeth on the roof of the mouth are in two lines. The general color of the trout is olive-brown or golden, and it has a somewhat reddish hue along its sides. In males at breeding time, the belly tends to be red or vivid yellow.

The subspecies of Cutthroat found in the Yellowstone River *(Salmo clarkii lewisi)* have been planted in many of the smaller lakes near the timberline. Here, too, we face a considerable variation in the coloring of fish, but the slash mark on the throat will always identify it as a variety of Cutthroat.

Cutthroats of the same species often present striking differences in color and physique when found in separate waters. I have found at least six different body colors and different shapes among the "black-spotted" trout, which can grow to a length of thirty inches in streams near Chama.

Spawning

The spawning season of the Cutthroat is quite variable. In Wyoming, they spawn in spring and summer; in Idaho, spawning begins in April and ends in late June. Like other trout, the Cutthroat selects its breeding grounds in the shallow riffles of clear streams. Only very occasionally does the female build more than one nest. As with most trout, once the eggs are fertilized by the male, the redd is covered with gravel. Spawning is usually completed in two days and the hatching takes from forty to fifty days. Small fish, or alevins, after absorbing the yolk sac, begin feeding seventeen to thirty days after hatching. One two-year-old hatchery hen fish yielded three hundred seventy-two eggs, whereas heavier fish have been known to yield from three thousand to five thousand eggs.

The Cutthroat feeds on insects, small fish, plankton, fresh water shrimp, crayfish, and terrestrial insects. Some of the finest waters for angling for Cutthroat are in the Yellowstone National Park and its environs, including northern Wyoming and Jackson Hole. In rivers near the sea, Cutthroat trout are migratory and will venture into the salt water for a period of time, only to ascend their parent stream again for spawning purposes.

GOLDEN TROUT (SALMO AGUABONITA)

This fish, never large but of rare beauty, inhabits the waters of the high country.

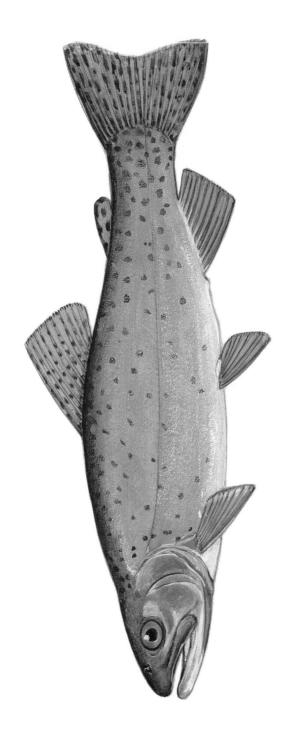

Cutthroat Trout (*Salmo clarkii*)

The average length of the Golden is from eight to twelve inches, but if the food supply is plentiful, they may grow up to eighteen inches. At elevations above nine thousand feet, the food supply is usually sparse. Originally from California's High Sierras, these fish have been transplanted throughout the higher mountains of the West.

The Golden trout grows slowly: about one inch the first year, a little over five inches in the first two years, eight inches in three years, and about ten inches in five years. Goldens have a diet that consists mainly of insects, insect larvae, small crustaceans, and occasionally smaller fish. (It must be mentioned that there is another trout, also called a Golden trout, which should not be confused with the Kern River Golden or White trout that live in the East and are found only in a few lakes in New Hampshire and Maine.)

In the West, fishing for Goldens has intrigued many an angler. The angler can fish only after the snow in the mountains melts, must climb to high altitudes, and must suffer cold nights and rough country. As a reward, the angler takes only a few fish, but is satisfied to have taken trout out of almost inaccessible locations and to have cast in waters that are as close to heaven as anyone can get.

Physical characteristics

The typical Golden trout is a brilliantly colored fish. The dorsal surface is light olive with a rose-colored lateral band from head to tail, and a bright orange or yellow band on the belly. The dorsal fin is tipped with an orange hue, and the ventral and anal fins are tipped with white. Some dark spotting may occur in the area of the caudal peduncle. Many retain their parr markings; others substitute spotting for the parr stripes. There is considerable variation in the coloration of the Golden trout from one lake to another. In some lakes the fish lose their parr marks and spottings, while in others, older fish may become brown on their back surfaces. In higher altitudes, they can be a brilliant yellow color, whereas in the lower reaches, the colors are more somber.

Spawning

These trout spawn from early June to July. The number of eggs produced by the hen fish may vary from three hundred to one thousand. Spawning takes place in trickles of shallow water or in shallow shore areas of the lake or pond. The incubation period is twenty days at 58°F.

CHARR TROUT
(SALVELINUS)

BROOK TROUT (SALVELINUS FONTINALIS)

The Brook trout, a charr, is sought after by many fishermen. There are many species of charr, including the Brook and the Dolly Varden. The principal charr trout of the Rocky Mountains is the Western Brook trout. Brook trout need cold, pure, turbulent water and, as civilization encroaches upon their domain, the Brookies vanish. Primitive areas are known for large, difficult-to-net Brook trout. Formerly, this species was variously known as the Eastern Brook trout, the Speckled trout, and the Squaretail.

Small streams yield small fish, whereas larger streams, ponds, and lakes can yield exceptionally large fish. If there is a waterway, many will migrate to and from the sea, returning up the streams to spawn. At this point, some Brookies can weigh as much as ten to fourteen pounds. Average sizes, of course, vary from one area to another, depending on food supply, aeration of the water, and the length of the growing season. The life span of the Brook trout has been said to be between eight and nine years. Maturity occurs from two to four years. The Brook trout is generally non-migratory. A top-condition Brook trout in cold northern waters is truly an artistic creation.

Physical characteristics

The Brook trout is the "salmon-like fish of the springs" and has adapted itself to most of the fishing waters in the United States. Since it requires a high oxygen level, it seeks well-aerated water.

The color of the Brook trout may vary from dark in older fish to a more brilliant color in younger fish. Many Brook trout living near the surface have a tendency to a blackish coloration, and blind fish are usually always very dark. No angler yet has caught a blind, or partially blind, trout in a mountain stream that was in good physical condition: the fish were usually starving because they lacked the ability to find food.

The scales of this fish are so small that most fishermen believe that Brookies are a fish *without* scales. The back is mottled and there are many pale yellow or grayish spots on the sides, or small red spots with a halo of light blue. The Brook trout's pigmentation will vary according to the degree of light and color of the surrounding water and vegetation. In dark, cavernous places where the sun fails to strike, the fish will have very few red, yellow, or orange spots on their bodies, and in some cases, the skin may develop a light, almost albino color. They can be very dark in amber waters, whereas in sparkling meadow streams they are often silvery. Regardless of the special circumstances, the abdominal fins will always have the distinctive white or light bands on their anterior, or forward, surface. This obvious white edge is important in identifying the common Brook trout. During breeding season, the male will have a burst of crimson or orange along the lower sides of his belly and perhaps a spray of black just above it.

The eye of the Brook trout is large, the head big but not long, and the snout somewhat blunt. The Brookie is favored with a large, cavernous mouth, the upper portion of which reaches back well behind the eye. The tail (caudal fin) is square. This fish lives and thrives in water temperatures not exceeding sixty-five degrees.

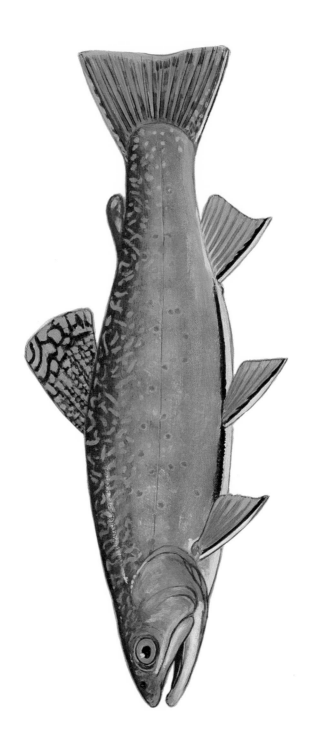

Brook Trout (*Salvelinus fontinalis*)

Spawning

During the autumn months, Brook trout constantly seek higher reaches of water for spawning; otherwise, their spawning habits are similar to those of the salmon family. If the water becomes warm, they will continue farther upstream. Driven by their reproductive instinct, they will leave warmer pools for colder pools in higher riffles.

When Brook trout reach the spawning grounds in late August to October, the female shapes her nest in sand or gravel in about six inches of water, fanning it clean with her tail and removing large pebbles with her mouth. During spawning, the male fish approaches the hen fish and rubs his body on hers. She then enters her nest, ejects a few eggs, and the male fertilizes them. This process continues over and over again until all of the eggs are fertilized, after which the exhausted fish leave the nest.

It has been calculated that not more than five percent of the eggs hatch. Most of the destruction is caused by minnow and sucker fish who have a great appetite for trout eggs. Young females produce two hundred to five hundred eggs, whereas the older females produce up to three thousand eggs. The incubation period, at 50° water will be between forty and fifty days, or twenty-eight days at 60°. When spawning season is over, Brook trout go downstream to deeper water, sometimes as much as fifty miles from the point of spawning.

The Brook trout's diet consists mainly of insects, larvae, worms of all types, nymphs, fresh water shrimp, and other crustaceans. They will rise to all manner of small objects floating downstream, nose the object, may even seize it, then spit it out and turn tail on it. A Brook trout will often spit out an artificial lure so quickly that one wonders if it even had a chance to taste it.

DOLLY VARDEN *(SALVELINUS MALMA)*

The Dolly Varden ranges from northern California to northwestern Alaska, and eastward to Idaho and parts of Montana. Its appearance varies greatly from one place to another, but the characteristic anterior white line of the pectoral and ventral fins is always present. The dorsal fin has an olive color.

Although the new nomenclature refers to the Dolly Varden as *Salvelinus malma,* the older literature refers to this same fish as *Salvelinus parkei,* and many naturalists, to complicate the problem, claim that this trout is the same as the Arctic charr, *Salvelinus alpinus.* Interestingly, it is impossible to tell the difference between these fish if one takes into account the great variations that occur quite naturally.

The story has it that the name Dolly Varden was given to this fish by the wife of a hotel keeper on the Sacramento River, who upon seeing the fish for the first time, exclaimed, "Why, it is a Dolly Varden!" an allusion to the variegated garb in which Charles Dickens clothed one of his heroines, a coquettish girl wearing cherry-colored ribbons. (The reference is to one of Dickens' lesser-known works, *Barnaby Rudge*.)

The record Dolly Varden was taken in 1949 and weighed thirty-two pounds and measured some forty inches. It was caught in Lake Pend Orielle, Idaho. Regardless of size, the Dolly Varden is an excellent game fish and is a challenge to any angler. It will fight like a Brook trout, is a stout sport fish, and is a gastronomic delight.

Physical characteristics

In general, the Dolly Varden resembles the Brook trout, but the differences are easily distinguished. The color of the dorsal surface is olive, the sides are sprayed with pale red and orange spots, and there are no vermilions on the sides, as occur to a greater or lesser degree in the Brook trout. The fins have no spots, but the white line on the anterior aspect of the ventral and pectoral fins exists, as is the case with most charr trout. Regardless of variations in color, the dorsal fin is always olivaceous. Unlike the inland species, sea-running Dollies are often slim and silvery.

Spawning

Spawning usually takes place in streams in the fall and early winter. Dolly Vardens spawn in shallow water over a gravel or stony bottom. They feed primarily on insects, crustaceans, smaller fish, and the eggs of other fish.

LAKE TROUT *(SALVELINUS NAMAYCUSH)*

The Lake or Mackinaw trout is a charr, and is probably the largest member of the trout group of Salmonidae. It is a superb food fish and is presumably a fine game fish. I have never fished for Lake trout and most of the information that I have is from various fish and game officers.

Lake trout occur in deep, well-aerated lakes and reservoirs, where water temperatures average 55° during the summer months. The fish usually range near the bottom, in water depths from fifty feet to over one hundred feet, except in the early spring and late fall, when they can be found at depths ranging from five to thirty feet.

These fish are relatively slow-growing, but often exceed thirty pounds in weight in many Colorado lakes and reservoirs. They may live as long as forty years, but older fish are seldom taken; in the twelve to twenty-inch size range, they are easier to catch compared to larger fish. An abundance of forage fish is necessary for Lake trout populations. They do well in lakes and reservoirs that contain Kokanee salmon, suckers, and other species.

In northern lakes in the Yukon Territory they appear more abundant than elsewhere. An eighty-seven-pounder was taken in Canada in 1906, and more recently, a one hundred and two-pound specimen was brought out of Lake Athabasca in northern Alberta and Saskatchewan.

Lake trout are hatched and reared artificially in Colorado's cold water units, such as the Estes Park Unit. The fingerlings are planted in several lakes and reservoirs scattered throughout the state.

Physical characteristics

The body color of the Lake trout varies widely. In general, shades of gray and olive predominate. Much of the body is mottled with light gray or white spots, and vermiform tracings cover the back and head. It has a deeply forked tail.

Spawning

Lake trout spawn once each year, October through November; the spawning period may range from a week to a month. There is no nest building; rather, they spawn over rocky areas on wave-swept shoals, at water depths ranging from a few inches to one hundred feet. The female lays about three thousand eggs. Most mature at five to eight years of age. Fish sixteen inches in length average about one pound in weight; eighteen-inch fish average two pounds; twenty-inch fish, two and one-half pounds; twenty-two-inch fish, three and one-quarter pounds; twenty-four inch fish, four and one-quarter pounds; and so on. Add a pound for every additional three to five inches in length.

GRAYLING
(THYMALLUS THYMALUS; THYMALLUS MONTANUS)

Some of the most interesting fish in the Salmonidae family are the several species of grayling. The extraordinarily large dorsal fin, almost a sail, can always be clearly noted. There is also no mistaking a grayling when it has taken a surface fly: this fish rises *perpendicularly*. Unlike other trout, it will not come to the surface in an arching motion; rising swiftly and vertically from their bottom position, it will often leap over a floating fly and take it on its downward motion. They are definitely leader-shy, and this shyness accounts for success in down-stream, rather than upstream, casting. Wet, dark-hackled flies and nymphs are effective, as the grayling's diet consists mainly of tiny mayflies and other small flies. Another of its curious habits is to follow the fly before taking it, so that a brief time lag is involved. The upstream fly moves too quickly and may not earn a fish. In the downstream method, a slack line is indicated and often, cross-stream quartering is successful. Thus, placing flies on the surface where one has seen a grayling rise must be done with precision.

The grayling favor the high-altitude streams of the Beaverhead and Big Hole country (I have taken many on the smooth waters of the Big Hole above the Wise River). There, in the land that Chief Joseph and his Nez Perce followers surrendered after their final battle and that Lewis and Clark explored while searching for a route west, this fish thrives and increases in numbers.*

In regard to the flavor of the cooked fish, Bergman expressed a high regard for it in the closing chapter of his book, *Trout*:

> As a morsel of food, the grayling is the most appetizing, by far the best freshwater fish I have eaten. The flesh is firm and has a distinctive flavor, and [is] much better eating than trout.

The Montana grayling is somewhat the same in external characteristics and behavior as the trout and charr; its primary difference is skeletal, as the structure of the skull and antipleural spires on the anterior ribs differ from either of the aforementioned.

Physical characteristics

Graylings have large scales compared to other trout. All species and subspecies of *Thymallus* have a huge, sail-shaped dorsal fin that carries seventeen to twenty-four rays. This fin is flecked with either bluish, blue-green, gray, lavender, or silvery spots. Spotting may also occur behind the operculum. The color of this fish varies with the intensity of light, and can change hourly: sometimes the color is a metallic sheen, at other times silvery, lilac, or golden. The grayling is a fish of great beauty and has received praise over the centuries.

The body is oblong, the mouth delicate and small. The jaw is short, extending just past the center of the eye. The teeth are sparse on the jaw structures, the vomer bone is short and contains a small patch of teeth, and the tongue has virtually no teeth. The air bladder is enlarged out of usual proportion. The adipose structure is slender and small, and the tail is distinguishably forked.

Spawning

Thymallus reaches its optimum spawning period in April and May, depending on weather conditions. It produces between two thousand and three thousand eggs per fish. In the past, egg production was much greater than this, but the fish are smaller now. The grayling in the Big Hole River of Montana, for example, run about ten to thirteen inches.

Observers have reported that grayling build actual depressions or nests. The males establish their territories in suitable spawning grounds and then defend the area against other males. Spawning occurs in shallow areas so that the backs of the males and females are out of the water.

---

*Unfortunately, the grayling was essentially eradicated in another of its North American habitats, the waters of Michigan; the causes were overfishing and the lumbering industry which, through the floating of logs down rivers, raked the spawning beds and destroyed the eggs and young fish.

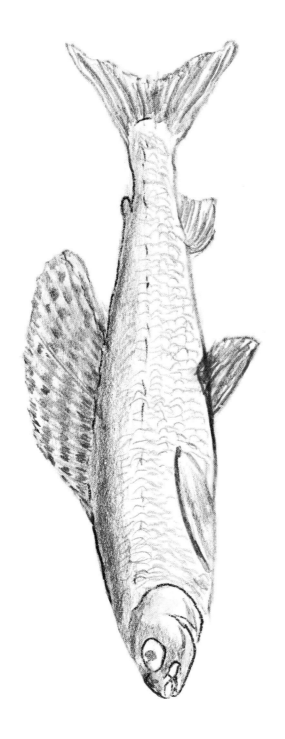

Grayling (*Thymallus montanus*)

The male meets intruders with his dorsal fin erect, but folds it over the back of the female during the act of spawning. Their bodies tilt upward and they begin to vibrate, this motion causing a depression in the sand. The fertilized, adhesive eggs drop into this slight cavity in the stream floor. Sand and gravel then cover the depression.

Compared to trout, grayling males produce a small amount of milt. This makes hatchery operations difficult, but the efficiency rate has been very good. Grayling hen fish appear to spawn often, either with the same male or with several males. Spawning sometimes involves two males, and may occur at any hour of the day. The optimum spawning season usually occurs in April or May, depending on the weather and temperature. It would appear that very cold water is required.

KOKANEE SALMON
(ONCORHYNCHUS NERKA)

The Pacific salmon are all of the genus *Oncorhynchus,* and within this genus are five species. *Oncorhynchus nerka* is well known in Pacific waters as the Sockeye salmon, and ranks as one of the world's major food supplies. Its flesh is red, rich in flavor, and quite suitable for canning. Salmon exist in large numbers and are taken with nets by commercial fishermen.

Once this salmon is transplanted to favorable landlocked waters, the situation changes and it becomes a most desirable lake sporting fish. There is a great demand for more fish in lakes and reservoirs and this salmon is quite suited to most bodies of water, although, for unknown reasons, they occasionally fail to adapt.

The Kokanee has many names including Little Silver-Sides, Silver trout, Little Red Fish, Kennerly's salmon, and Kickaninny. In Idaho they are called Blue-backs and are taken by trolling or spinning lures. There are, as usual, several minor varieties of no great importance.

This little fish is an excellent fighter, and tastes delicious when fried or poached. Kokanee have been introduced in Oregon, Washington, Idaho, California, and throughout the entire Rocky Mountain area.

Physical characteristics

The Kokanee salmon is a small, land-locked form of the Sockeye salmon. It reaches maturity in two to seven years, depending upon the strain. From lakes, this little one-to-two-pound fish migrates upstream or to pools and shallow, protected portions of a lakeshore.

As spawning approaches, the male Kokanee develops a hooked jaw and a humped back, the body turns a deep red color, and the face and tail turn a deep green. Before these spawning changes, the Kokanee may closely resemble a Rainbow trout in appearance. Fishermen can distinguish between these two fish by counting the rays in the anal fin: the Rainbow has twelve or less, whereas the Kokanee has thirteen or more. Before maturity, black spots become predominant on the head and back.

The spawning female is much less gaudy. There is some coloration on the female, but even this is quite variable. Immature fish are usually a brilliant color, although sometimes they are drab yellow, with silver sides. The dorsal surface of this fish can be either light or dark green, with tiny black specks.

Spawning

Spawning takes place in the autumn of their fourth year, usually in October or early November, and after the spawning episode they die, characteristic of most Pacific salmon. The young hatch in forty to fifty days, then move from the streams or lakeshore to deeper waters.

In spawning, the fish ascend the streams and males and females pair off and defend the nest; their breeding and nest care is similar to that of the trout. The female Kokanee will stay over the nest until death overtakes her, which may take from twelve to fifteen days.

Kokanee salmon have made a total adaptation to freshwater migration without returning to the sea. Even a few of the Atlantic salmon, which return to the sea after spawning, can adapt to land-locked conditions.* It is significant that the Kokanee is making a decisive and permanent adaptation to land-locked waters. The major problem, of course, is that when this small fish reaches full maturity and ascends a stream to spawn, it dies. Because of this, smaller streams often contain either exhausted or dead fish.

Kokanee salmon were introduced in Colorado in 1951. Since that time, female and male fish have been caught in traps during the spawning season. These traps are set by the Fish and Game Department in small streams. The hen fish are stripped of their eggs and milt is obtained from the males to fertilize the eggs.** Each female produces from six hundred to eight hundred and fifty eggs, which, once fertilized, are raised into fry for restocking purposes.

---

*Lake Vaner in Sweden, for example, which is completely isolated from the sea, possesses a stock of land-locked, non-migratory salmon.

**Between Lake Herron and the Elvado Lakes in New Mexico flows a stream that is a continuation of the Chama River. There are great pools alongside the stream that in October fill with Kokanee. From one such pool, I took several female fish and placed them in a smaller pool some fifteen feet away from the river; gently squeezing the females, I convinced them to drop several hundred eggs in gravel nests. After coercing the male fish into depositing milt over these eggs, I then covered the nest with fine gravel. My hope was, of course, that when the spring run-off occurred, the young parr would be pushed into the mainstream and avoid being gobbled up by their parents. In one or two cases, the procedure seemed to work, but I fear that my impromptu breeding program had a poor percentage of success.

Whitefish (*Prosopium williamsoni*)

WHITEFISH

(PROSOPIUM WILLIAMSONI)

Our interest here, the Mountain whitefish or the Rocky Mountain whitefish, is highly regarded by some anglers and dismissed by others. It is found from the Rocky Mountains to the coastal streams, and north to British Columbia. Northern Wyoming absolutely abounds with these fish.

The whitefish of the Rocky Mountains is essentially a cold water fish. The nomenclature is somewhat confusing regarding different varieties. For instance, the shallow water whitefish is called a Cisco or a Lake herring, the deep water ones are called chubs, and the round or torpedo-shaped fish are called inconnee. There are also many subspecies, and as a result, no clear-cut categories can be distinguished.

The food of the whitefish varies with its environment. It may surface feed, depending on the available insects. More often it will feed off the bottom on nymphs and other aquatic insects, often rising to flies. Plankton also forms a good part of its diet. The whitefish is an excellent sport fish and is also good to eat. The flesh of this fish lends itself nicely to brine soaking and subsequent smoking; smoked Whitefish is a true delicacy. Marinated whitefish is also a gastronomic delight.

Whitefish can be taken in cold months when other fishing is difficult. Many consider the whitefish a pest that takes food away from the trout. Therefore, it has been recommended that the whitefish population be controlled. In my opinion, however, this would not be a good idea, as angling for whitefish is gaining popularity.

Physical characteristics

The whitefish's lower jaw is shorter than the upper jaw, and the mouth has no teeth. For this reason, the fish is sometimes called a "sucker" fish. The slender body is a slate grey-blue with silvery sides. The underbelly is usually white. When mature, these fish vary in size from fourteen to thirty inches.

Spawning

When living in lakes, whitefish usually move upward into streams to spawn in October and November. Spawning in high, cold country, on the other hand, can take place as early as August or September. The ideal temperature is from 40° to 45° F. Spawning is a nocturnal activity for whitefish, and takes place over gravel beds in riffles.

The whitefish become mature at two years of age, with sexual maturity occurring at three years of age. The yield of eggs is from fifteen hundred to twenty-five thousand. Usually, the eggs require several months to hatch; however, if the water temperature is from 50° to 55°, the period of incubation can be shortened to between thirty-six and forty days.

OTHER SPORTING FISH

SUNFISH FAMILY

SUNFISH *(CENTRARCHIDAE LEPOMIS)*

The sunfish family is one of the more popular groups of sport fishes in the United States. A large number of fresh-water fishermen confine their interest to the pursuit of sunfish.

The American Fisheries Society lists some thirty species of sunfish, but many subspecies and varieties are also recognized. These warm-water fish are native to our continent. The sunfish family consists of fresh water bass, true sunfish, Rock bass, and crappies. They are excellent for schooling young fishermen: I have taught many a child the technique of angling by using sunfish for the trial-and-error early period of angling life. Sunfish have a tendency to overpopulate a body of water, though, and when large numbers are present, the food situation can become precarious. In this situation, the fish remain small, making the sport of angling difficult and frustrating. All sunfish, though bony, are delicious when fried or otherwise properly prepared.

Sunfish generally have a deep, compressed body. The dorsal fin is rather spiny and is contiguous with the second dorsal fin. The anal fin also holds spines, and the tail is broad and strong. From a lateral aspect, they appear rather flat. There is a remarkable variety in their choice of water, from warm to quite cold. These fish are spring and summer spawners and use shallow depressions, excavated by the males, for nests. The males also guard the nest, and occasionally herd or protect the young when hatched. The adult fish feed on insects of all kinds and even small fish. The young feed on microscopic organisms or aquatic invertebrates.

Crappies and certain undefined Rock bass are "true" sunfish. They can be scrappy little fish but most of them receive scant attention from the more adroit anglers. It should be noted that there are many varieties of crappies and sunfish. Additional information on these fish can be found in Beckman, William C., *A Guide to the Fishes of Colorado* (Boulder: University of Colorado Museum), 1952, Leaflet Number 11; and Reid, Jess T., *Fishing in New Mexico* (Alburquerque: University of New Mexico Press), 1956.

The Largemouth and Smallmouth bass are truly game fish, but the smaller sunfish, particularly the bluegills, can also be excellent rod-and-reel fish. In fact, the bluegill can be a fine sporting fish for anglers using dry flies.

LARGEMOUTH BASS *(MICROPTERUS SALMOIDES)*

The Largemouth bass is a popular fish, found in relatively warmer waters. Huge quantities of Largemouth bass are caught throughout the South, Southwest, and Midwest. Besides being taken in lakes or in the Rocky Mountains, they are taken in ponds, often mixed with bluegills.

There appear to be two types of Largemouth bass: the more northerly *(Micropterus salmoides salmoides)* are differentiated from the ones taken in Florida—the Southern or Florida bass *(Micropterus salmoides floridanus)*. The northern can be distinguished by its lateral line scales, which number from sixty-one to sixty-six, and above the lateral line, number from seven to nine; the scale rows usually number from ten to thirteen.

The Largemouth ranges from Canada south into Mexico. I recall a pond near Scottsdale, Arizona, that was literally filled with these bass. Aside from plugs and flies, a piece of red rag on a hook could easily have taken one.

Physical characteristics

Largemouth bass grow to considerable size, adding about five to six inches a year. In the previously mentioned Scottsdale pond, they weighed eight to ten pounds; in more southern waters they can grow up to fifteen and sixteen pounds. Although a record fish of twenty-two pounds has been reported, the northern bass do not achieve such dramatic growth; in colder climates, hibernation inhibits growth.

The Largemouth has a patch of small teeth on the tongue; in fact, the tongue of the Largemouth feels like sandpaper. Other distinguishing marks are from three to four lavender streaks radiating from the eye across the gill cover. The ear spot, which is about the same size as the eye, is a dark brown. The eyes appear somewhat red in color. There are mottlings in the rear of the dorsal fin and on the tail. Unlike the Smallmouth, the bands or bars of pigment on its sides run horizontally. This fish is found in many of the streams and ditches of the Pecos

Largemouth Bass (*Micropterus salmoides*)

and Rio Grande waterways. It is less desirable than Smallmouth for flavor. Its adaptability to sluggish waters has encouraged its introduction into many ponds, reservoirs, and slow-flowing streams. The great increase in dam building has also created ideal water for the Largemouth bass.

Spawning

Spawning takes place in late winter and early spring in the South, and later in the northern waters. Temperature appears to be a controlling factor, with spawning occurring ordinarily at between 64° and 73°. Sudden drops in temperature may kill the eggs or the newly hatched alevins. Spawning takes place in sheltered waters of from two to six feet deep, the male making the depression for the eggs and carrying away small pebbles in his mouth. The adult fish fans the eggs, thus eliminating silt that may otherwise settle on them. The female will carry from two thousand to thirty thousand eggs and, at water temperatures of 66° or more, the eggs will usually hatch within a week.

The male defends the nest with great pugnacity against any intruders. Young bass feed principally on aquatic insects, while the adults' food consists of small fish, crustaceans, snails, insects, worms, frogs, tadpoles, and crayfish. The fry grow rapidly, attaining increases in length of three inches in five months, and five to six inches in one year; by their third year, they have often reached twelve inches or more. Largemouth bass feed incessantly. The best possible time to fish for them is early morning or early evening.

The Largemouth bass is often by water weeds and beds of water lilies; when fishing for Largemouth bass, one should cast to waters adjacent to water plants. He has a keen sense of smell and will often refuse to take dead bait. It is therefore quite interesting that this fish will strike at artificial lures. The primary function of the lure when dealing with bass at its action: it must be made to move to and fro because when the lure is motionless, bass rarely strike. A two-pound bass taken on the surface with a large floating fly will put up quite a fight before exhaustion occurs.

SMALLMOUTH BASS *(MICROPTERUS DOLOMIEU)*

The Smallmouth bass, like the Largemouth, is a top-ranking gamefish and is eagerly sought after by anglers. In my experience the Smallmouth bass puts up a greater battle than the Largemouth bass. This is particularly true in wild running water. This fish goes by several names. It has been called the Black perch, Tiger bass, Bronze bass and (erroneously) Striped bass. It has been found in most of the waters in the United States and Canada. In 1950, these fish spread into the New England states.

Stream areas dotted with boulders and pools between riffles are favorite

Smallmouth Bass *(Micropterus dolomieu)*

45

locations for this fish. They also prefer clear, fast water over rocky areas. Those living in dark water are of a darker hue, while those in bright, sandy water are of a lighter color.

The Smallmouth bass has a very spinous dorsal fin that is not as light as that found in the Largemouth. The mouth is quite large (why they are called "smallmouth" baffles me). The upper jaw does not extend to the back and sides. It is interesting to note that when spawning the females have vertical blotches and contrasting colors. However, a good deal of color variation exists.

A distinguishing characteristic is that the general pigmentation of the Smallmouth consists of vertical bars, whereas in the Largemouth fish such bands run horizontally. Another distinction is that when the mouth is closed, it reaches almost to the eye of the fish. In the Largemouth, the lining of the mouth extends considerably past and behind the eye.

With the advent of cold weather the Smallmouth bass becomes less active, feeds less, and retreats into deeper waters. In the latter part of November it ceases to feed and hibernates until early spring. Studies have shown that the required water temperature for hibernation is 50° or lower.

Spawning

The Smallmouth bass is a spring spawner, from April to June. Ideal water temperatures for spawning are from 60° to 65°F. Male and female spawn more than one time and not usually with the same mate. Nest building is more or less similar to that of the Largemouth bass; the male constructs the nest and guards the eggs and the young. A bottom that is composed of gravel, coarse sand, or bedrock is nearly always selected.

Egg production varies from about one thousand eggs in a twelve-inch female to ten thousand in larger fish. The eggs hatch quite quickly: within two days in water temperatures of close to 80°, longer in colder water. With abundant food, the fish grow rapidly.

It seems to me that the Smallmouth eats anything that moves, from floating insects to submerged crayfish. Smallmouth bass fishing, using surface plugs, can be a wonderful sport. The Smallmouth has the untiring strength and bravery usually attributed to trout. The greatest pleasure is taking these fish with surface lures and light tackle.

BLUEGILL (LEPOMIS MACHROCHIRUS)

The bluegill is probably the most common, and best known, of the sunfish. It originated in the Great Lakes and was later found in the Mississippi Basin and in Florida, and is now found throughout the United States. Many other names have been given to the bluegill, including bream, brim, copperhead, sun perch, pumpkinseed, and blue sunfish. When taken on a light rod, the bluegill is a

Bluegill (*Lepomis machrochirus*)

scrapper. Since the fish has a relatively small mouth, it must be struck quickly, setting the hook.

Physical characteristics

The bluegill is easily distinguished from other types of sunfish by its long, sharp pectoral fins and black "ears." The body is flat, deep, and broad. The upper part is dark olive and blue-green, while the lower part of the abdomen or belly can be yellow, brown, or blue-green. The mouth is relatively even, and is located well before the eye. The fish is called bluegill because of the blue color on the lower sides of the head.

The ear flap has a flexible rear edge and is broad and dark on its margin; there is no red spot. A somewhat dark area is present on the middle portion of the second dorsal fin. The front of the belly is colored either orange-yellow or orange-red. This is particularly noticeable in breeding males. Vertical, colored bars are present on the sides of living fish.

A record bluegill of some four pounds has been reported. Ordinarily, bluegill can overpopulate a pond or lake, but control is usually maintained through the consumption of young fish by bass and other predators. Bluegills multiply rapidly in any pond because they are hardy and sustain with impunity the many insults of weather and nasty water conditions.

Bluegills travel in schools. If one is caught, others are usually taken in the same area. It should be noted, however, that schools of bluegills will travel rapidly from one side of a pond to the other. They tend to gather around brush or other water weeds, and will often seek the shade of an overhanging tree or bush. They are easily frightened.

Spawning

The number of eggs produced by a spawning female will vary from twelve thousand to fifteen thousand, depending on the size of the female. Spawning takes place in late spring or early summer. Nests are made in shallow water over sand or gravel. There are usually twenty to forty nests around the shoreline. The male builds the nest on the diameter and they can be clearly seen because there is a rim of sand or silt around the hollow structure. Often, more than one female will lay her eggs in a nest and the male will keep the nest clear by the gentle motion of his fins. At the same time, after fertilization of the eggs, he will guard the nest against intruders. A large number of bluegills hatch and a great many survive.

BLACK CRAPPIE *(POMOXIS NIGRO-MACULATUS)*

The Black crappie has a wide range of distribution; it is found from southern Canada to Florida and throughout the West. The early plantings of these fish from the East occurred in Seattle's Lake Washington, in 1890; in Lake Cuyamaca,

Black Crappie (*Pomoxis nigro-maculatus*)

49

White Crappie (*Pomoxis annularis*)

50

near San Diego, in 1891; and in Idaho and Oregon in 1892 and 1893, respectively. From these areas, the fish spread in all directions as they increased in numbers.

The Black crappie prefers clear, weedy lakes and large streams. It may be distinguished from the White crappie by the number of spines on its dorsal fin, numbering either seven or eight instead of six. Apart from this difference, the Black crappie and the White crappie can be quite similar. The Black crappie is a handsome fish with habits generally very close to those of the Bluegill.

WHITE CRAPPIE *(POMOXIS ANNULARIS)*

Like most crappies, the White crappie has a compressed form. The dorsal fin rarely contains more than six spines. The lower jaw projects from a somewhat large and oblique mouth and extends to the rear of the eye. It is quite ubiquitous, found in streams and reservoirs. Spawning occurs in summer, usually in deeper water; redds are prepared in gravel. White crappies appear to travel in schools and can be taken on wet flies, bugs, and dry flies. Fishermen who use spinners can catch a bucketful once they locate a school of these fish.

REDEAR SUNFISH *(LEPOMIS MICROLOPHUS)*

This little pan fish is found only in a few areas in the Rocky Mountain region. The pectoral fins are about one third the standard length of the body. I have seen only two specimens from the Pecos area and do not regard the Redear as a true sporting fish. It has been planted in the Pecos waters and is not indigenous to the territory.

LONGEAR SUNFISH *(LEPOMIS MEGALOTIS)*

The Longear sunfish is a relatively uncommon fish found in the quiet, weedy water of the lower Pecos and Rio Grande valleys. The soft dorsal and anal fins are tinged with orange, while the back has an olive hue. As a game fish, it is of limited importance. In over forty years of fishing, I have never seen a specimen.

PERCH FAMILY
(PERCIDAE)

WALLEYE *(STIZOSTEDION VITREUM)*

The most singular fighting fish of the Perch family, and one of America's better known sporting fishes, is the walleye. It is principally a lake fish and thrives best in large bodies of water, but has been found in larger streams. In New Mexico, it is limited to several lakes, one of these being Lake Maloya. It is known by many names: Golden pike, Yellow pike, Jack salmon, Opal eye, and Dore.

Aside from the sport of catching this voracious creature, walleyes are an excellent food fish. The flesh is not fatty or oily, and it makes an excellent freezer fish. It is usually taken by spinning lures, trolling, and still fishing with live bait. I have attempted to take one at night on salmon streamers with flies and large nymphs, but the traditional heavy flies just gave me a tired arm and severe frustration.

Fifty years ago, whole trainloads of walleyes, or Perch pike, were shipped from Canada to American markets. Even to this day, large quantities are imported, for the walleye is a highly flavored fish and few anglers will deny that this is the best reason for catching them. A walleye for dinner is a culinary event.

Physical characteristics

The walleye has an elongate, slightly compressed body. There are two dorsal fins, the first composed of spines, the second of soft rays. The mouth, when wide open, gives the impression that it could swallow anything; it is the mouth of a predator and has large, pointed teeth lining the jaws. In every way the mouth resembles that of a true pike of the more northern waters. The name Walleye pike is derived from the nature of its mouth and the somewhat cloudy appearance of the eye.

The general coloration of the body, particularly the upper parts, is a mottled brown that grades to white on the belly. Along the back are several dark blotches, which resemble saddle marks, rather than the typical crossbars of perch. Pelvic fins are usually white or a yellowish hue, and there is a white tip on the lower lobe of the caudal fin.

These fish spend most of their daylight hours in the depths and surface in the shallows at dusk or in darkness. They are entirely carnivorous, feeding on other fish and sometimes on frogs. They mature in two to three years. Thus, their growth is rapid, the females becoming larger than the males. There are, of course, variations in growth rates; the average size is from fifteen to twenty inches, but larger fish have been reported.

The lifespan is approximately seven to eight years. One interesting feature of the walleye is that they are far-ranging. Tagged fish have been recovered after traveling one hundred miles in a single month. In short, walleyes really have no home base, but go about hither and yon, looking for food. Whether winter or summer, they appear to be always feeding.

Spawning

From the beginning of April to sometime in May, walleyes spawn. This takes place at night in shallow waters, at temperatures of 43° to 63°F. The eggs are deposited over gravel, stones, or lake bottom rubble. In shallow water, males and females are sometimes heard splashing about, or "roiling." Spawning usually

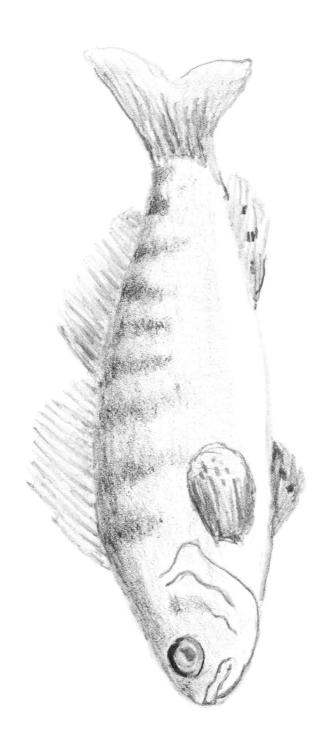

Yellow Perch (*Perca flavescens*)

takes place over a three-week period; there is no parental care of the spawning grounds or later, of the eggs. The eggs are small, fertilize easily, and the yield is roughly one hundred forty thousand eggs per quart. Large females have been known to lay six thousand eggs. Incubation lasts twenty-six days at 40°, or shorter if the water is a bit warmer.

YELLOW PERCH *(PERCA FLAVESCENS)*

The Yellow or ringed perch is a popular and prolific fish that takes baited hooks eagerly. It is an important food fish and is taken in large numbers by anglers and commercial fishermen. As a table delicacy, it is highly desirable. With its yellow coloration and the seven dusky bars that cross the back and sides, it is easily identifiable.

This fish thrives best in clear, weedy lakes or ponds, and eats insects, crustaceans, fish, snails, worms, and other fauna. Yellow perch are usually bottom feeders, but in the fall of the year they can be taken with flies. What is of importance is that these fish will not take a dry fly, but only a submerged fly. The fly must be moved under the surface to gain the attention of the fish.

Since the Yellow perch multiplies at a great rate, many states have increased creel limits. In overcrowded lakes and ponds, or in unusually warm water, the perch become infested with parasites. Various species of worms form cysts in the muscle beneath the skin. The parasites are not harmful to humans and are easily killed by cooking.

Physical characteristics

The lower fins of the adults tend to be red or orange. There are two dorsal fins, the second containing three spines and twelve soft rays. No enlarged teeth are present.

Spawning

These fish are random spawners and do not construct nests or care for their young. The eggs are laid as a mass, with a somewhat stringy consistency, and are draped over aquatic vegetation or sometimes marginally submerged in sand and gravel. The eggs average twenty-five thousand to thirty-five thousand to the quart, the quantity depending upon the size of the female. Eventually the male appears and fertilizes the eggs.

CATFISH FAMILY
(ICTALURIDAE)

There are many species of catfish, six of which are common to the Rocky Mountain area and southern New Mexico. They are nocturnal, omnivorous, bottom feeding, and they find their food by chemical senses. All species of catfish are edible; they are often skinned and cut into filets. Catfish fries are received with enthusiasm wherever catfish fishing is in vogue.

In the Rockies of New Mexico, two types of catfish are common: a small form, native to the Pecos and certain parts of the upper streams and ponds, and a larger form, native to the Canadian River. These larger ones have been transplanted to all of the southern Rockies and throughout the state of New Mexico, including west of the Continental Divide, where catfish are not native. The smaller of the two, *Ictalurus lupus*, has a more deeply forked tail and twenty-five or more rays in the anal fin.

Catfish feed in the main channels of a stream, or anywhere food is available, during twilight hours. Most catfish are found in slow water, such as sluggish areas of lakes and rivers. Catfish can thrive in almost any place, and can stand pollution better than most fish. They seem to be more active at night, and begin serious eating just after dusk. Tenacious, they will fight to stay alive even out of water for a considerable length of time, particularly if covered with wet weeds or grass.

The adults may reach a length of thirty inches and a weight of twenty-five pounds, but individuals over ten pounds are rare. Rod and line, and set lines or trotlines are often used, the hooks baited with a variety of substances (set-line fishermen jealously guard their formulas).

BLACK BULLHEAD *(AMEIURUS MELAS)*

In western waters, particularly in New Mexico, the Black or Dark bullhead is the most common catfish found in lower, warm-water lakes. It is native to northern New Mexico and is most often found on a mud bottom in small ponds, creeks, and canals.

Black bullheads travel in schools. The adult has a black hue, with black chin barbels, and the anal fin is shorter than those in other catfish, with between seventeen and twenty-two rays. The sides of the fish are plain, not mottled.

Like most of the other catfish, the bullhead spawns in spring and summer. The females deposit their three thousand to four thousand eggs in saucer-shaped depressions made by the male, who guards the eggs. Bullheads rarely exceed a weight of two pounds. The bullhead is easily taken with worms during the warmer months.

The Black bullhead has a wide distribution, ranging from Hudson Bay to the Great Lakes, and west and southward to Colorado, Kansas, and Wyoming. In northern New Mexico, west of Abiquiu, there are large populations of various catfish.

YELLOW BULLHEAD *(AMEIURUS NATALIS)*

This catfish is easily distinguished from other catfish by its white or cream-colored barbels (slender, tactile projections near the mouth). The tail fin is more

Brown Bullhead (*Ameiurus nebulosus*)

rounded and less notched, and the anal fin has from twenty-four to twenty-seven rays. The coloration of the upper parts is somewhat of a green hue or is slightly yellow-tinged. The anal fin has two longitudinal bands. This fish is not indigenous, but has been introduced in several ponds and streams. I first came in contact with this fish in the lower portion of the Gila River.

Commercially, it is of minor importance. The adults vary from five to fifteen inches in length, with an average weight of twenty-one pounds or less. They are excellent pan fish, and as such are welcomed by most anglers.

BROWN BULLHEAD *(AMEIURUS NEBULOSUS)*

This fish has been introduced into certain waters of New Mexico, Colorado, and other areas of the West. It also goes by the name of Speckled bullhead, Horned pout, and Squaretail catfish. It is now present in weedy ponds and small lakes containing abundant vegetation.

Brown bullheads have sharp, pointed spines on their dorsal edges and pectoral fins. The anal fin contains twenty-two to twenty-four rays. The fish's color is olive to brown, with dark mottlings on the sides. The barbels range in color from gray to black. Most species average from eight to ten inches in length, and weigh about a pound. Their spawning activities and eating habits are similar to other catfish, with maturation taking three years. These fish are considered a tender delicacy.

FLATHEAD CATFISH *(PYLODICTIS OLIVARIS)*

The Flathead is another large, river catfish. It has commercial value and is taken on trotlines with as many as fifty hooks being used at one time, although it is also sometimes netted. Other names given to it are Shovelhead, Yellow cat, and Mudcat. It should be noted, when comparing these fish to other catfish, that the Flathead is entirely carnivorous. On trotlines, pieces of meat or worms are often used as bait. In New Mexico, they are found primarily in the Rio Grande, Pecos, and Gila watersheds and have been introduced into many western streams.

The size of the Flathead is related to the amount of food available. Favorite fishing spots include deep holes and pools. Most of these fish weigh from two to five pounds, but fish from twenty to forty pounds have been taken by surprised anglers. Insect larvae, crustaceans, and other fish make up most of their diet. Maturity is reached in three to five years. Spawning takes place in late spring and summer, and the female yields from five thousand to ten thousand eggs, which hatch within twenty to thirty days.

These fish are firm-fleshed and have a delicate flavor. The Flathead grows large and makes a fine table food.

PIKE FAMILY
(ESOCIDAE)

NORTHERN PIKE *(ESOX LUCIUS)*

The Pike family of North America consists of four species: Pickerel, Redfin pickerel, Northern, and Muskellunge. Members of this group can be found all over the world. However, since it has been introduced into quite a few lakes in Rocky Mountain and northern New Mexico waters, we are concerned primarily with the Northern pike.

The Northern pike is of holarctic distribution, ranging across northern Europe, Asia, and North America. It is a vicious carnivore and it seems to me that it will eat anything that moves. The reports of the stomach contents of these fish are of particular interest. They eat other fish, mice, crustaceans, insects, small ducks, frogs, crayfish, and carrion. The creature simply has a voracious appetite. Its introduction into trout waters can be disastrous to the trout.

Physical characteristics

The sides of the Northern pike's head and body are covered with pale, elongated spots or blotches on a background of dark green. Dark markings are typically present on the tail and the fins, but there can be considerable color variation in these fish. The Northern pike has a fully scaled cheek. The average length of the Northern pike is from twenty to thirty inches, and the average weight is between fifteen and twenty pounds. A pike of forty-six pounds, and fifty-two and one-quarter inches in length, has been recorded.

An interesting feature of this fish is that it will shed some of its teeth and renew them. They do retain an efficient set of teeth at all times. The roof of the mouth bristles with teeth and they are also found in the tongue. Aside from the already mentioned destruction of waterfowl, the Northern pike will gobble up mice, rats, frogs, leeches, crayfish, and other strange fish that venture forth.

Spawning

Spawning begins in early spring and the female lays thousands of eggs at random. The waters selected are inlets, ditches, and swampy areas. The hen fish is usually accompanied by several males. The eggs are adhesive and cling to any submerged vegetation. Large females have been known to deposit ten thousand to two hundred thousand eggs a year and the incubation period lasts from fourteen to thirty days.

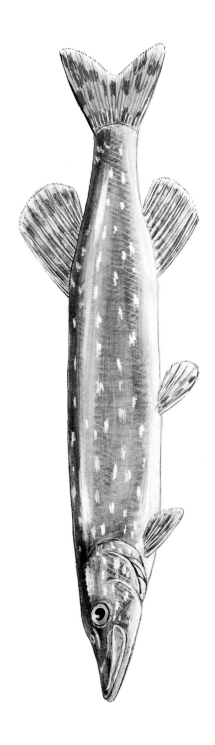

Northern Pike (*Esox lucius*)

MINNOW FAMILY
(CYPRINIDAE)

The Minnows are the largest group of freshwater fishes. Most of them are not game fish, the goldfish and squaw fishes being classic examples. (In Oregon, the Umpqua squawfish is also known as a whitefish.) The Minnow family includes shiners of all kinds, chub, bonytails, and many others. Perhaps the one that has received the greatest attention is the carp. Many a leader I have broken in an effort to retrieve a large carp. The struggle that these fish put up is unbelievable.

CARP *(CYPRINUS CARPIO)*

The carp is a large, significant member of the Minnow family. Fish culturists recognize several varieties of domesticated carp. In Europe, they were considered a delicacy when properly marinated and smoked. There have been madrigals composed, woodcuts made, and legends written about the carp.

The carp is an Asiatic fish, introduced from China into Great Britain and continental Europe in 1227, when the Romans still occupied Europe. For centuries, they were gourmet table fish and were selectively cultivated in ponds. In 1872, they were introduced into North America. By 1877, the carp craze was in full swing and by 1894, most rivers of the West supported large populations of these fish; even the Snake River in Nevada had plenty of them.

Carp exist in many Colorado and northern New Mexico waters. There are three main types, one fully scaled (called scaled carp), another with irregular scales mainly in the lateral and dorsal regions (known as mirror carp), and finally one which has no scales or only a few (called leather carp). They are really the same species.

In much of Europe, carp are raised commercially. They are the largest source of animal protein that can be produced in an acre of water. Although in most places in the United States the carp is considered a pest, I have never found it so. My only objection to the carp is that it will not take a fly, and therefore my objection becomes a prejudice. Such prejudices are unfortunate, for I enjoy eating carp when it has been well prepared. Marinating for several days in wine, herbs, lemon juice, etc., is a prerequisite to a fine baked specimen.

Physical characteristics

The carp is a robust, muscular fish, deep through the body. Three varieties exist, varying from heavily scaled to those having practically no visible scales at all. The carp may resemble its relative the goldfish, but the goldfish has no barbels as the carp does. Its mouth is moderate in size and is toothless. The barbels are in pairs on each side of the mouth. The carp is easily distinguished from other

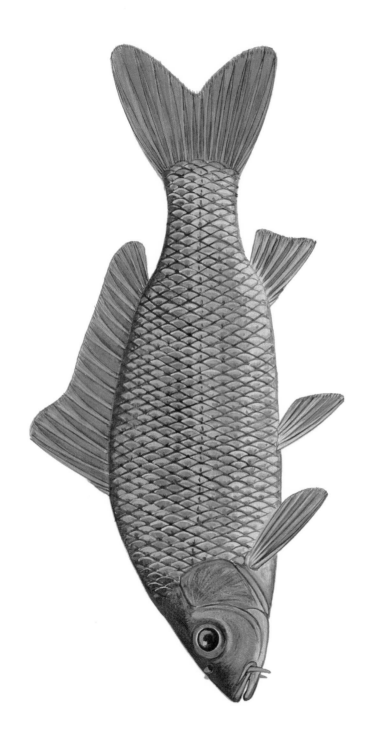

Carp (*Cyprinus carpio*)

members of the Minnow family by its long dorsal fin with a long, serrated spine. Leather carp, without scales, have been misnamed Carpsuckers and Buffalo fish.

This fish is abundant in warmer waters: lakes, ponds, canals, ditches, and some rivers. The carp is essentially a vegetarian and multiplies profusely. They devour plants, roots, tubers, and algae, and, on rare occasions, worms, insects, crustaceans, and fish eggs. Like many bottom feeders, carp tend to roil the water. When alarmed, they seek shelter in holes. In early spring, carp appear in the shallows, enjoying sun bathing. In winter, hibernation takes place in the bottom of lakes. Favored bait includes dough balls, worms, kernels of sweet corn, and even stale pieces of hardened doughnuts.

The adult fish has a bronze hue, with olive green on its back. Most of the fish taken are from five to ten pounds, but twenty-five to fifty-pounders are not uncommon. A ninety-pound specimen was caught in Switzerland in 1825. The rate of growth is rapid and is dependent on the food supply.

Spawning

Spawning takes place in late spring and summer: May, June, or July. The fish seem to have little fear during spawning. They move onto lake shallows and marshes, and the eggs are scattered at random over plant beds and rubble.

The female will deposit five hundred to six hundred eggs in an area of about five to six feet in diameter. The grey-white eggs, of about two millimeters in diameter, are somewhat adhesive and stick to plants or to the bottom. The males seem to fertilize these eggs without much regard for the process. The eggs will hatch in about five to twelve days, depending upon water temperature. In four or five days, the yolk sac is absorbed and the small fish can speedily swim into hiding places in the water weeds.

CONCLUSION

Quite often I have wispy clouds of recollection. I may be alone on a stream that sparkles with melodious movement; in the wind, golden arcs of line and leader reflect a setting sun. Sometimes I find myself remembering companions and conversations on some trout stream of long ago. Or I recall the thoughts that I had while fishing—pleasant ones—listening to the sounds of birds and the splash of trout. There are similarities between fishing and philosophy. In fishing, as in life, *it is well to cast far enough, accurately enough, and delicately enough* for any situation. The gently aimed, thoughtful approach is often best.

The process of fishing is a particular one and with the ability to cast a light, artificial fly, the event becomes extremely personal. The great joy of taking difficult fish is an experience never to be forgotten and the ramifications of fishing are endless. "Less equipment and more knowledge" is a good rule of thumb. All of the advertised paraphernalia in the world for catching fish will not replace the carefully studied cast. The graceful arcs of line and well-placed flies or lures require continued training and thought. The experienced fisherman knows when to rest fish. He avoids the continued sweeping of a stretch of water, and he knows, for example, that game fish have excellent vision and can be very easily disturbed.

As I come to the end of this little book, I hope that it will prove to be a practical reference for anglers, and, if so, I will have come to the end of a perfect self-imposed assignment.

SUGGESTED READING

The list of those who have written treatises on their avocation includes many individuals aside from Dame Juliana Berners (*A Treatise on Angling,* 1486), Izaak Walton (*The Compleat Angler, or a Contemplative Man's Recreation,* 1653), Joseph Brooks (*Trout Fishing,* New York: Harper & Row, 1956), Preston Jennings, Peter Oliva, and various members of the Orvis and Leonard rod companies. One of the most scholarly fishermen was John McDonald, who wrote *The Complete Fly Fisherman: The Notes and Letters of Theodore Gordon* (New York: Theodore Gordon Flyfishers, 1970). Another important reference is Roderick Haig Brown, *Fisherman's Fall* (New York: William Morrow and Co., 1964); Haig Brown left his British Columbia home many times for winter fishing trips to the Argentinean and Chilean waters. A detailed look at the variety of fish and eels in the United States and Alaska is Edward C. Migdalski's book, *Freshwater Sportfishes* (New York: Ronald Press, 1962); this book includes lampreys and many others not considered to be game fish. Its primary value is that it includes all the fish that can be caught in this country. Finally, I must recommend Edward R. Hewitt's book, *A Trout and Salmon Fisherman for Seventy-Five Years* (New York: Scribners, 1948).

Other books not to be overlooked are Charles Wetzel, *Practical Fly Fishing* (Boston: Christopher Press, 1943); A. Gingrich, *American Trout Fishing* (New York: Stackpole Books, 1951); Vincent Mariner, *A Modern Day Fly Code* (New York: Brown, 1950); Ray Bergman, *Trout* (New York: Knopf, 1938); Ernest Schwiebert, *Trout,* 2 volumes (New York: Dutton, 1978); and G. E. M.

Skues, *The Way of the Trout with the Fly* (London: n.p., 1921). The latter is a classic reference work.

The publications on fish in the French language are even greater in number than those in English. Of particular value is the work by P. Barbellion, *Truite, Mouches, Devons* (Paris: Librarie Maloine, n.d.); a book of over 1,100 pages, this has become the bible for fishermen, a classic in every respect. In my opinion, it is the most comprehensive book ever written, and is nicely complemented by Charles Ritz's book, *A Fly Fisher's Life* (translated from the original French and issued by Crown Books in 1959, 1965, and 1972).

A complete listing of all the books on angling and fish would be encyclopedic. I have just presented favorites from my libarary shelves. It can only benefit the reader to investigate and acquire his own valued references.

INDEX

References to illustrations are printed in boldface type.